Making Things and Teaching the Creative Arts in the Post-Digital Era

This interdisciplinary book critically studies the processes of making art and creative arts education in the post-digital era.

Drawing from fields such as Philosophy and Pedagogy, it demarcates a meaningful understanding of what it is to make art and things, and to teach artmaking in this contemporary landscape. The book develops and articulates a phenomenology of aesthetic practices within the post-digital era and covers themes such as the aesthetic practices of making and the experience of an aesthetic act through a digital interface. Chapters also suggest new didactic approaches to understanding and creating form as an integral part of creative arts education in the post-digital era, and analyses creative arts pedagogy research in this light. The experience of materials and space, both real and virtual, are presented for theoretical reflection throughout the book.

This book will be of interest to scholars working in aesthetics, art, design, public art/public space, art education, digital culture, and human-computer interaction studies.

Ellen Marie Saethre-McGuirk is Professor of Art and Design Education at Nord University, Norway.

Making Things and Teaching the Creative Arts in the Post-Digital Era

Seeing and Experiencing the Self and the Object through a Digital Interface

Ellen Marie Saethre-McGuirk

Routledge
Taylor & Francis Group

LONDON AND NEW YORK

First published 2022
by Routledge
4 Park Square, Milton Park, Abingdon, Oxon OX14 4RN

and by Routledge
605 Third Avenue, New York, NY 10158

Routledge is an imprint of the Taylor & Francis Group, an informa business

British Library Cataloguing-in-Publication Data
A catalogue record for this book is available from the British Library

Library of Congress Cataloging-in-Publication Data
Names: Saethre-McGuirk, Ellen Marie, 1975– author.
Title: Making things and teaching the creative arts in the
    post-digital era : seeing and experiencing the self and the object
    through a digital interface / Ellen Marie Saethre-McGuirk.
Description: Abingdon, Oxon ; New York, NY : Routledge, 2023. |
    Includes bibliographical references and index.
Identifiers: LCCN 2022013641 (print) | LCCN 2022013642 (ebook) |
    ISBN 9780367333515 (hardback) | ISBN 9781032340661 (paperback) |
    ISBN 9780429326264 (ebook)
Subjects: LCSH: Art—Study and teaching—Philosophy. | Art and
    computers.
Classification: LCC N84 .S24 2023 (print) | LCC N84 (ebook) |
    DDC 776—dc23/eng/20220517
LC record available at https://lccn.loc.gov/2022013641
LC ebook record available at https://lccn.loc.gov/2022013642

ISBN: 978-0-367-33351-5 (hbk)
ISBN: 978-1-032-34066-1 (pbk)
ISBN: 978-0-429-32626-4 (ebk)

DOI: 10.4324/9780429326264

Typeset in Times New Roman
by Apex CoVantage, LLC

In memory of my dad, Arild Ove Sæthre, whose love of building, engineering, and cars inspired my love of making things, constructing things, and enjoying the beautiful things in life.

Contents

Figures

Preface

This book rounds off a major theme that I have been working on since 2015, through both traditional research and research-based artistic practice; that is, arts education in the digital field and artistic practice in digital space. In many ways, it is simultaneously a starting point for my continuing work on and in digital space. In light of many teachers and researchers having both gained significant experience with online learning and experiencing the subsequent increased push towards digital tools in education due to COVID-19 risk-reducing strategies, it is time to analyse how we can use these tools to make better, stronger, and more sustainable plans to include them, moving forward post-Coronavirus. But what is more, I believe that multidisciplinary and cross-disciplinary research and humanities-based innovation in practice is the key to moving our local, national, and international communities forward, enabling us to think afresh about the central problems and issues we have to solve. As such, I believe that this and future work on digital space, creative innovation, experience, and visual art is not only relevant, it is necessary.

Preliminary versions of parts of this book were presented as papers at conferences throughout the Nordic countries and in Australia from 2016–2018. My first paper on the topic, titled 'Traversing Neo-Luddites and Technophiles', was an unpacking of the phenomenological particularities of working in the virtual versus the real, given at the 'Make it Now – Learning, exploring, understanding' conference at The University of Turku, Finland, in September 2016. My second paper on the topic, titled 'Wink's Axe', was given at the 'Dybde i kunst og håndverk' conference at the Oslo Metropolitan University (OsloMet) in Norway, in January 2017. 'Wink's Axe' was inspired by the artistic research by university lecturer Magnus Wink from the University of Umeå, Sweden. Following this, I gave the paper 'Smooth, Silent, and Inodorous – Arts Education in the Digital Field', at the e17 conference at Umeå University, Sweden, in October 2017, where I delineated what the digital brings with it in terms of learning in and through the arts with regards to arts education. The last paper, given in 2018 as a seminar at the Design Lab, Queensland University of Technology, in Brisbane, Australia, was titled 'Experience and Understanding through Digital Innovations'. I would like to thank all of the conference organisers for allowing me to present my work on digital space, as well as my fellow conference attendees for inspiring discussions.

Acknowledgements

I would like to express my sincere appreciation to Mr. Morten Edvardsen and Mr. Gisle Pettersen, both of the Faculty of Education and Arts, Nord University, for the many opportunities given to me and for their support. I would also like to express my appreciation to my digital art and design education colleagues for their support, especially this past year, and to my students at Nord University, who have been eager discussion partners on teaching and learning in the creative arts in digital space.

I would also like to offer my special thanks to the academic community at the Design Lab at the School of Design, Creative Industries Faculty, at Queensland University of Technology, Australia, and in particular to Prof. Dr. Evonne Miller, Director of the QUT Design Lab, and Dr. Glenda Amayo Caldwell, Program Leader of Design Robotics and Digital Fabrication. The remainder of the book was developed through seminars and papers given while I was a Design Lab Visiting Fellow in 2018. The Design Lab community is truly unique as a trans-disciplinary academic community and a catalyst for new thinking. In addition, I would like to extend my thanks to Dr. Caldwell's project team at UAP, in Brisbane, Australia, who together with Dr. Caldwell graciously demonstrated their exciting work in the field to me in June 2018.

I am especially grateful to my family; in particular to my husband Prof. Dr. James Nicholas McGuirk for being an essential dialogue partner and critical reader, as well as to my mother, Mrs. Ella Jørgine Sæthre, for all of her help while I have been writing. This book would not have been possible without them.

Lastly, I would like thank Emilie Coin at Routledge for her generous patience and support throughout this process.

Author biography

Ellen Marie Sæthre-McGuirk (Ph.D., Katholieke Universiteit – Leuven, Belgium) is Professor of Art and Design Education at Nord University (Bodø, Norway). Previously Director and Head of Research at the Norwegian National Center for Arts and Culture in Education, Director of the Rogaland Museum of Fine Arts, and Associate Professor II in Museum & Gallery Leadership studies at BI Norwegian Business School (Oslo, Norway), she has until recently taught digital art and design education in in-service teacher education. She is now Head of Secretariat of the Norwegian Competency Network for Student Success in Higher Education, and heads the Digital Arts Lab research group at the Faculty of Education and Arts. Furthermore, she is also currently Section Editor of the Youth Engagement and Education section of the Journal of Public Space, and Editor in Chief of the Nordic Journal of Art and Research, both of which are open access online journals.

Sæthre-McGuirk has a research-based art practice, with an anchoring in pedagogical artistic research, and extensive experience as curator and art critic. In addition to her academic background in Photography, Art History, and Mass Communication, Sæthre-McGuirk completed her master's degree in European Studies with emphases on modern European Cultural History, Human Rights, and EU law at the Katholieke Universiteit in Leuven, Belgium, in 1998, where she also later defended her Ph.D. in Philosophical Aesthetics and modern Art History in 2003. Her research interests include higher education; art education and pedagogy; museums, museology, and audience development; and innovation, digitalisation, and the creative arts.

1 Introduction

The digital in the creative arts

Like many academics working in visual art and art education, the diverse and physical hands-on experience of making art and things and studying materials and objects played an important part in my academic upbringing. Reflecting on those hands-on experiences of making is a sentimental past-time. Memories of sharpening my paintbrush between pursed lips (before the age of health and safety standards in the studio) or spending days waiting for and seemingly watching clay dry to that calming, cool leathery texture, offer a wealth of insight into things and the materials that they are made of. Granted, it is not just about touch. Tactile experiences blend with the experience of other sensory qualities during the act of making. As important as the feel or sight of it are the experienced smell, weight, size, resistance, and sounds of things and their materials.

These sensations and the perception of them make up my communication with the materials; a communication which seems essential for making art, both in terms of giving form to an import through the materials while in the act of making and in the physical, more practical terms of being able to use the appropriate tools to form the material at hand. Tools as such are an extension of my hand, and I form, move, and undertake operations on the material through them. I perceive the material and the effect of my actions on it through my extended perception of the materials' qualities.

To illustrate what I mean by this, consider the following act of drawing: When drawing, the sound of a pencil's graphite and clay binder pushing up against paper gives you a greater and richer experience of both the paper and the pencil, as well as the act of drawing. Concentrating on the pencil, you can both hear and feel where the pencil tip's graphite and clay mix touching the paper is more solid and hard or more porous, as one pulls or pushes the pencil on the paper. And as the pencil dances across the paper's fibres, the pencil itself must be twisted, turned, and angled so that the line becomes

DOI: 10.4324/9780429326264-1

what is hoped for or intended. Concentrating on the paper, the attentive drawer will experience the qualities of the paper as both sound and force of friction pushing against the pencil as the pencil itself is pushed. The sound of the pressure of the pencil reverberates through the weight of the paper, the structure of its fibres, and the tactile qualities of its surface. The sound resonates; sometimes into a soothing monotone rushing sound, other times into a quick and brutal saw-like beat. Concentrating on the line drawn, this sensory information feeds the thoughts and reactions of the one who draws, a millisecond before the act has taken place and that single decisive moment has passed. The drawing becomes a succession of such single decisive moments, which only become a significant form pregnant with import and artistic permanency when the drawer is capable of internalising this sensory information, not only in the act of drawing, but also in the moments before the act of drawing will take place. The individual drawing is thus not only a chronicle of this internalisation; it is also a testimony of time and of experience. The individual drawing serves as a witness of the succession of moments and actions, tying this notion of time and experience into the concept of drawing or making things.

Compared to making art in the real world, working through digital interfaces is an abstract undertaking. Drawing with my digital pencil, I am inadvertently making two drawings. One, by my pared-down and thus near-universal drawing implement which, on its own, leaves no physical trace on an inflexible and unchanging surface that is perfectly smooth and oddly quiet. This drawing exists only in my mind's eye. The other, beyond the surface, where a line by any conceivable drawing implement can be mimicked, any paper qualities can be imitated, and the scale of my drawing in relation to me can be modified to fit nearly whatever need may be. Digital tools and materials lack physical qualities compared to tools and materials in the real, and in this light, both the interface and the act of making there seem strange.

The amalgamation of visual and subdued auditory information offered to me by the surface interface imitate those from real materials and are as such merely stand-ins, awkward prostheses intending to substitute and extend the digital's disadvantaged physical link to the real world. The two-dimensional digital interface is relentlessly smooth and monotone when I draw on it, underplaying all other senses for the benefit of the visual. Only through intense concentration do I become aware of its idiosyncrasies, impoverished as they are. Yet, my digital pencil and surface remain unapologetically just that, and any visual characteristics of my line belong more to the mute software than the hardware. I have a writing tablet, too, and while its user interface tries to mimic the porous surface of paper, it is unyieldingly exclusively that. Its porousness is uncanny. Three-dimensional digital interfaces fare no better. They fail at simulating a physical space shared with me, partly because those objects have no sounds inherently their own. They do not give off or reflect sound and therefore do not claim space. Furthermore, there is no weight to the digital objects I form, so the objects there convey nothing in relation to how they sit in the space beside me. When I touch them, those objects do not resist or give rise to a sensation of temperature change in comparison to my skin, leaving them wordless when it comes to articulating the material's transient pliability and malleability.

In the end, I cannot communicate with materials in the act of making digitally because there are no materials to communicate with. The things I make on my tablets and in virtual three-dimensional space are in this sense mere reflections of physical drawings and things with no qualities of their own. None that can be seen and experienced, at least, and then felt and checked in the same action. None that can link up to and be rationalised by their origins. These digital things want to trick me, it seems. They are dishonest and unfaithful to materials and the experienced world in their making. The digital works themselves are untainted by their own deceitfulness, though; they are content orphans from physical origins. I am somewhat reminded of their disconnect when they are transitioned into the real world by being printed or produced. The digital works are then made strangely unfamiliar to me by taking on new and different physical and sensory qualities. The works are nevertheless mine. Unabashed in their new physical form, they claim space by my side, often without demonstrating a need for my analogue habits or my sentimental musings about materials and making.

The problem with this arguably unnecessarily negative portrayal of a loveless relationship with the digital is that not only do I digitally make things, such as forms that have it in them to become sculptures or drawings in or through digital interfaces, but professional praxes have long included digital tools in their working processes, too. Clearly, that exemplifies that creativity continues, things can still be made, and we can still think and make ideas into being by using digital tools. Indeed, from a purely practical point of view and as illustrated earlier, the relationship between materials and makers has changed significantly with the emergence of digital tools, interfaces, and materials. But that does not mean that the profoundly human act of making things has ceased to exist in the digital field.

With this in mind, how is it, then, that we can make things in or through the digital sphere if giving form to objects is dependent on communication with materials? What of the rich and diverse overlapping space between the two outer points of the reality-virtuality continuum, embracing degrees of augmentation in both directions of the continuum? Does materiality take on different roles or become inessential in this regard? Some digital things are made in and for digital space, others are intentionally made in digital space to one day step into the real world. And, while others again are made in the real and will remain in the real, we increasingly take advantage of digital tools and interfaces when handling them. As such, digital space spanning the reality-virtuality continuum is an especially interesting space in that it puts any understanding of what creating in the post-digital era is or can be to the test.

In an attempt to embrace making in our post-digital era, we can question whether the act of making is necessarily diluted or muted in the digital sphere. Or, should we rather say that the act of making things digitally is not diluted, muted, better, or worse; it is simply different. The more interesting question, then, is what are the essential and non-essential differences in making in the post-digital era, and why are these so? It is a difficult question. While the interface certainly obscures and stunts my yearning for communication with physical materials, it also demands its own way of communicating during the act of making things in virtual space, on digital platforms, and through other digital tools; things which do not yet, or may never, exist in the real world. This difference has significant implications for making in digital space and for teaching in the creative arts, as it is present in early childhood education, school, and higher education as art and visual art, as well as in a number of related professional programmes and fields. Beyond asking how this making can play out in digital space, I also ask what this means for teaching it.

The post-digital era

I have specifically used the term 'the post-digital era', as opposed to 'the digital era'. With the term 'post-digital', I lay special emphasis on how not only new technology but also new forms of interaction and action enabled by that technology have changed or challenged central areas of our creative and social lives. One presentation of the term 'post-digital' in relation to teaching that is relevant for this book can be found in Paulo Boa Sorte and Cristiane Vicentini's discussion on educating for social justice:

> [T]he new forms of interaction facilitated by technology make frontiers between the virtual and non-virtual increasingly imprecise. As we are led to different ways of relating to one another, ubiquitous communication has impacted teaching and learning in the diverse contexts and knowledge areas.
>
> (Boa Sorte & Vicentini, 2020, p. 201)

It is exactly that imprecise frontier between the virtual and non-virtual and ubiquitous communication that is brought to the fore in my use of the term 'post-digital', along with the implications that follow regarding our ways of relating to the world around us.

To further unpack this term, we can look closer at Florian Cramer, who Boa and Vicentini relied on in this regard, and his 2015 explanation of the 'post-digital' as 'a contemporary disenchantment with digital information systems and media gadgets, or a period in which our fascination with these systems and gadgets has become historical' (Cramer, 2015, p. 13). Even more to the point, however, we can attend directly to Cramer's anecdote of a young hipster sitting on a park bench and writing on a mechanical type-writer to help us better understand the term 'post-digital':

> In 2013, using a mechanical typewriter rather than a mobile comput-ing device is . . . no longer a sign of being old-fashioned. It is, instead, a deliberate choice of renouncing electronic technology, thereby call-ing into question the common assumption that computers, as meta-machines, represent obvious technological progress and therefore constitute a logical upgrade from any older media technology – much in the same way as using a bike today calls into question the assump-tion, common in many Western countries since World War II, that the automobile is by definition a rationally superior means of transporta-tion, regardless of the purpose or context.
>
> (Cramer, 2015, pp. 12–13)

Cramer continues to list a number of tools that have been recently resur-rected as post-digital devices, such as vinyl records and analogue photog-raphy. But as Cramer then expounds, the term 'digital' merely means that 'something is divided into discrete, countable unites – countable using whatever system one chooses, whether zeroes and ones, . . . tally marks on a scrap of paper, or the fingers' (Cramer, 2015, p. 17). Consequently, Cramer's post-digital stance in actuality dismisses the notion of universal machine, not digital things in their own right (Cramer, 2015, p. 19). The term 'post-digital' thus 'describes the messy state of media, arts and design *after* . . . the digitalization of crucial aspects of the channels through which they are communicated' (Cramer, 2015, p. 19). That is, the current state in which the digital disruption has already occurred, which rejects 'techno-positivist innovation narratives' (Cramer, 2015, p. 20).

The problem with this early stance on the post-digital is that the uptake of traditional tools can only be considered post-digital when they are repur-posed in relation to their newer, digital counterparts: 'vinyl as anti-CD, cassette tapes as anti-MP3, analogue film as anti-video' (cf. Cramer, 2015, p. 21). Or the old and the new is differentiated 'between shrink-wrapped cul-ture and do-it-yourself culture', seen in, for example, the maker movement

(Cramer, 2015, p. 22). These are all reactionary stances, either-ors. Ironically, they are arguably also a division of the sociocultural fabric of the world around us into discrete, opposable units. This leads us to question the status of the dismissal of the universal machine: Did they not protest the machine too much, to honestly say they were over it?

The hipster's repurposing of machines, and by extension the maker movement's makerspaces and fablabs, were arguably neither still digital nor fully post-digital, in essence. Instead, which to be fair Cramer does indicate (Cramer, 2015, p. 24), a more mature post-digital stance would be to look past binary divisions and dichotomies, having overcome the systems crisis (cf. Cramer, 2015, p. 25) that characterised early notions of the post-digital, and then choosing the technology which was best suited for the project. By getting past these early conceptions, as it were '[moving] beyond binary concepts such as analogue/digital or use/non-use as well as concepts such as the digital divide' (Thorén et al., 2019, p. 324), we can look afresh at technological use in a post-digital society, and perhaps even understand the post-digital stance as one of a technological use-non-use assemblage (cf. Thorén et al., 2019, p. 326).

With this viewpoint and in this contemporary landscape, the overarching aim of the book is to demarcate a meaningful understanding of what it is to make art and things as art and to teach the creative arts with an emphasis on visual art. As such, this book concerns both processes of making things and creative arts education in the post-digital era.

Ultimately both an analytical and critical study, it draws from such fields as Philosophy and Pedagogy from the point of view of the maker. At the same time, there is more to this discussion in that it is an interdisciplinary, detailed enquiry of the creative arts and visual art education, which is also nestled together with human-computer interaction studies. Therefore, the relevance of this discussion is not confined to only making art in the post-digital era. Parts of this discussion can be of benefit for fields concerned with any type of making and working through a digital interface, because as a study of a unique kind of human-computer interaction, it can help improve our understanding and thus, ultimately, the usability and functionality of computer interfaces. From a human-computer interaction perspective, this focus can uncover deep insight into user interface experiences, with a special emphasis on making through two-dimensional planes and virtual/augmented and mixed reality. The discussion as such concerns the physical interface between people and hardware, but equally concerns the experienced interface between people and software. A result of this work can be the re-imagining of the next generation of interfaces. Not so symphony orchestras can perform machine-composed pieces or artificial intelligence can paint portraits (cf. Ford, 2015, pp. 113–115), but rather so that the process of the maker making art and ideas and the way art and ideas are expressed can better take digital tools into service, enabling the further development of contemporary art practise. Additionally, any process that engages through or in virtual fields can better take digital tools into service, such as in medicine and health care, industrial development, safety, law enforcement, and military development. And in so doing, importantly, make transformative and radical innovation possible for both society and industry, as well as have an effect on the creative arts and art education.

The maker

I must offer some comments on the maker, who is the person whose actions are studied in detail throughout this book. I have intentionally steered clear of the term 'artist', as it seems to create unnecessary distance to children, youths, and young adults who engage themselves with artistic and creative activity, although they are not artists by profession and their work is rarely included in the corpus of Art History. Also, the term 'artist' can be understood as someone other than the designer or craftsperson. While there is a difference between crafting an object for specific use and artistic creation, that is not to say that artists cannot be engaged with a practice based on the making of objects of different kinds. Also, specific differences between art and design, as I will discuss later, are relevant, but not decisive, in light of art education. The term 'maker' is used as an attempt to sidestep all of these wayward discussions and simultaneously open up the book's discussion to other professions and activities also interested in human-computer interaction.

Following this, the term 'things', as opposed to 'art', is an attempt to include art made by children, pupils, and other non-professionals whose work is rarely shown at the art sector's apex institutions, such as art museums, galleries, and biennials. Not because their art process is any less an art process, but because the term 'work of art' can be considered more exclusive in a negative sense than the term 'thing' is inclusive in a positive sense. It is a difficult balancing act, made more complex by the need to not be too specific in terms of the particular materials and techniques used in the visual arts. For this reason, I have also attempted to steer clear of the term 'object', closely associated with the term 'art object', which is a highly regarded, unique, and often museum-based object. I admit, though, that it hasn't always been possible.

Therefore, my 'maker' is not necessarily a visual artist, even though I must admit that my maker is probably so. Nor is my maker necessarily a professional, although this level of conscious attentive interest in materials and making might be more familiar to a professional artist or art teacher.

I hope that my maker can also be recognised as the novice and the young who are addressing the making of things from the position of the pupil. So, to create space for a more accepting argument about making things and teaching the making of things which also encompasses that which is made in digital space by all of these, my argument builds on the maker, our need of a better understanding of what it means to make things through an art process, and what the implications of that are in terms of teaching in and about digital space. If we are to develop richer virtual environments and improve immersion or better our approaches for teaching in light of the post-digital era, we need to concentrate on understanding the maker's presence and action in making things.

Importantly, I am also the maker. Accepting that experience can be a source from which we can develop knowledge, the question is how experience can come to expression and how we can access it for critical review. Like Ståle Stenslie (2010) who took on an art-as-research project, I have found inspiration in the method of confessional writing for the study of practical, tacit knowledge:

> With this I practice writing in a first-person style where the author tries his utmost to describe the circumstances and finding of his research in a subjective manner. It is my intention as well as hope that the partially subjective descriptions in this work will expose my own and personal . . . path of building new knowledge within the arts.
>
> (Stenslie, 2010, p. 15)

I believe that this writing approach thus empowers readers to assess the role I play as both narrator and constructor of the arguments at hand (cf. Bardzell & Bardzell, 2015).

First-person writing covers a whole range of writing styles, from the more theoretically, mediated uses of the first-person such as in Phenomenology, to the literary, personal style. I admit that the nature of my topic necessitates an 'experiencing [that] is fully embodied, performed with the recognition of the intellectualism and the physicality of the experiencing self, as well as a strong sense of how experiencing is affected by specific circumstances' (Mah, 2008, p. 102), such as with Montaigne. Nonetheless, my approach is closer to the autoethnographical inasmuch as I allow my practical experience to frame the emergence of my critical discussion (cf. Hemelsoet, 2014; Tilley-Lubbs & Calva, 2016). This manages to be both personal and therefore intimate, but at the same time evaluative and critical because it draws out crucial and meaning-giving distinctions in this experience.

Through this approach and as my starting point I address the major areas of concern of this book: physical experience, experience of digital things and making, attentiveness in experience, and the pedagogy of making things in the post-digital era. Not primarily visual things, like the products of a graphic designer or even, to a certain extent, a photographer, who do not necessarily have the same type of physical presence and communication in the act of making with materials and beyond that other types of making art has, although these visual areas are interesting in their own right. Rather, my starting point is the creative arts where one intends to literally make things and things as art, virtual or real, which can also to a certain degree include designing and even industrial designing. It is interesting to note in this regard that even though they have long-established relationships with the act of making things through digital interfaces, mock-ups and clay models are still essential to the design processes in some of those fields. Such physical objects used for deliberation are still the ultimate touchstone for successfully thinking a thing through a creative process into existence alone or together with others.

Along the same lines of interest, the main argument of this book relates to divergent problem-solving and thinking through making in contemporary creative practice and learning. We are involved with those processes as they unfold in the post-digital era, making this study one which is of particular significance to those interested in the creative arts as a whole – both practice and pedagogy. While working with real materials and exclusively working in the real world has specific experience-based qualities not to be overlooked and working in and for virtual space has its own characteristics that are significant in relation to many making processes today, there is also a large and diverse creative space in between these two extremes. Its qualities and characteristics have significant implications for teaching, and to better understand these, we must demarcate the space where these processes take place and attempt to define the features that concern the self and the object, as well as seeing the self and making the object in digital space.

Therefore, from the perspective of our post-digital era, where much of the process to conceptualise, construct, and give form to things happens through a digital interface, my main argument concerns what happens when the making process in particular takes shape partially or as a whole on the other side of these interfaces and, subsequently, what our roles as teachers are in this regard. I simultaneously fully accept – and expect – that things can be made as art that do not have a form you can hold on to, such as sound art and works that take into service light or odours, let alone performance and other forms of art. Works such as those are less prominent in this book, even though I am hesitant to demand a strict division, because there is arguably a short distance in the process of making 'from the making of physical objects to the making of ideas and the way they are expressed', as Elliot Eisner argued (Eisner, 2002, p. 383). Aware of the unnaturalness of too strict a divide, I critically address what happens during processes of conceptualising, constructing, and articulating shaped space as meaningful form through a digital interface in an art process, and thus attempt to gain a greater understanding of the teaching-related implications of these processes as they take shape beyond the physical sphere. Furthermore, I do this by delineating a more productive understanding of the art process of making things through a digital interface, accepting that those processes are not merely one-way (human-to-computer), but have a retroactive effect on the person who is making the object (computer-to-human), as well as on the act of making itself.

Bibliography

Bardzell, J., & Bardzell, S. (2015). *Humanistic HCI*. Morgan & Claypool.

Boa Sorte, P., & Vicentini, C. (2020). Educating for social justice in a post-digital era. *Práxis Educacional, 16*(39), 199–216. https://doi.org/10.22481/praxisedu.v16i39.6374

Cramer, F. (2015). What is "post-digital"? In D. Berry & M. Dieter (Eds.), *Post-digital aesthetics: Art, computation and design* (pp. 12–26). Palgrave Macmillan.

Eisner, E. (2002). From episteme to phronesis to artistry in the study and improvement of teaching. *Teaching and Teacher Education, 18*, 375–385.

Ford, M. (2015). *The rise of the robots: Technology and the threat of mass unemployment*. Oneworld Publications.

Hemelsoet, E. (2014). Positioning the educational researcher through reflections on an autoethnographical account: On the edge of scientific research, political action and personal engagement. *Ethics and Education, 9*(2), 220–233.

Mah, H. (2008). The predicament of experience. *Modern Intellectual History, 5*(1), 97–119.

Stenslie, S. (2010). *Virtual touch: A study of the use and experience of touch in artistic, multimodal and computer-based environments* [PhD thesis, The Oslo School of Architecture and Design].

Thorén, C., Edenius, M., Eriksson Lundström, J., & Kitzmann, A. (2019) The hipster's dilemma: What is analogue or digital in the post-digital society? *Convergence: The International Journal of Research into New Media Technologies, 25*(2), 324–339. https://doi.org/10.1177/1354856517713139

Tilley-Lubbs, G.A., & Calva, S.B. (2016). *Re-telling our stories: Critical autoethnographic narratives*. Sense Publishers.

2 Creative arts processes

Making art and the role of art in life

To dig deeper into making as it relates to art and teaching the creative arts in both real and virtual space in the post-digital era, we can start by asking the fundamental, yet inherently complex question about how and why we make things.

We make things for a whole host of reasons, practical and personal, and sometimes even for no specific 'useful' reason at all. Furthermore, why we make things, how we make things, and the sophistication of the things we make change and mature over time. There are physical and cultural reasons for this, which are linked to our ability to understand and use objects as tools. A higher-order concept of function of objects develops in children at an early age, allowing both children and later adults to 'more readily organize, select, and communicate about hypothetical functions' of things (Deák, 2014, p. 167). Following this abstract concept of function and as a pre-requisite for tool-using innovations, the objects we make can in turn become tools in their own right, or take on completely different uses than initially intended. This specialised capacity is innately human, and it extends beyond our refined motor capacities and consciousness of the cultural context of object-usage, to include understanding the potential of dynamic human-object interactions (Deák, 2014, p. 149).

Spanning from naive exploration to the masterfully used object-as-tool, and from the serious to the whimsical end-product, there is arguably a central cognitive achievement which allows for all such tool-use and making things: namely, our ability to take notice of, remember, and flexibly imagine the many possible outcomes of intentionally using objects to cause different kinds of possible effects (cf. Deák, 2006). However, as we mature in age, we tend to acquire a design stance in relation to tools and objects; that is that we see, conceptualise, and understand things in terms of their intended or socially accepted function and through an interplay of purpose, function,

DOI: 10.4324/9780429326264-2

and design (cf. Dennett, 1987). Nonetheless, some actions and professions especially favour flexible thinking about object function and tool usage, such as engineering and design (Deák, 2014, p. 171). But also, arguably, making and perceiving art.

The early and assumingly lifelong ability to flexibly imagine the many possible outcomes of intentionally using objects to cause different kinds of possible effects relates to both making and perceiving art. Not only do we use tools and materials in artmaking that may or may not be used according to their intended function; often the maker takes advantage of flexible imagining and thinking about other things and their functions, too. A thing with a corresponding function-type, so to speak, can be seen out of context and repurposed. When Picasso lifted bicycle bars out of their context, paired them with an old bicycle seat, and created a bull's head, *Tête de taureau* (1942), he was skilfully manoeuvring between function, object, and representation. So elegant and clever was this coupling that in a study of Picasso's life and work, Roland Penrose said of the work that the metamorphosis was astonishingly complete (Penrose, 1981, p. 345). Penrose continued, 'Such transformations are a simple game, but for them to become significant it [*sic.*] requires a rare perception of the varied and subtle implications in the form in question'. Furthering this thought, Penrose referred in closing to a comment made by Picasso when the writer and ethnographer Michel Leiris had congratulated him on the transformation of the bull's head. Picasso had replied, 'That's not enough. It should be possible to take a bit of wood and find that it's a bird' (Kahnweiler, 1949, p. 7; Penrose, 1981, p. 345).

For the viewer, it is not interesting that Picasso with no visible effort had made this magical transformation astonishingly complete (cf. Penrose, 1981, p. 344). Simply turning some things wholesale into a bull and that new thing statically being a bull is not necessarily aesthetically interesting. Rather, it is the viewer's revelling in the uncertain and fluctuating identity of the object – now a bull's head, now bicycle parts, and now a bull's head again – that piques our interest in relation to that particular piece. In viewing *Tête de taureau*, our flexible thinking is brought to the fore, as the piece playfully invites us to exercise our ability to imagine an object's function and meaning: It is a bull and it is a bike; how is a bull like a bike and a bike like a bull? To take a bit of wood and find that it is a bird, or a pebble and find that it is a head of a dog or even a typewriter (cf. Penrose, 1981, p. 345), is in part to rediscover our exploration of objects and in part to engage our imagination. The resemblance between the represented (the wood and pebble) and the imaginary (the bird, dog head, and typewriter) can be slight, but the non-arbitrary iconic relationship between the two must nonetheless be there (cf. Casey, 1981, p. 150). As the viewer, these pieces jog our flexible thinking. Bringing the relationship to the fore and then hiding it again is the clever sleight of hand of the artist. A viewer coming to terms with the represented or the imaginary in and of itself and without flexibly shifting between the two would have the experience of that piece ruined for them.

Concentrating on the point of view of the maker, though, using this Picasso example seems unfair. It would seem to belittle the scope of which the call to flexibly think is present in even the most modest maker's art process. Not all pieces are as eloquent or as petite as *Tête de taureau*. And there is a lot more to art than just playfully revealing non-arbitrary iconic relationships. It is seeing, articulating, and expressing. Thinking through art processes and making art allows the maker to shift between the represented and the imaginary on a greater scale, inviting the viewer to join in on the discussion, as it were, at hand. What is more, the thing is not just a material starting block for imaginatively seeing or discussing; it is meaningful artic-ulation in its own right. In this sense, artmaking seems to be an advanced, embodied, multimodal process that results in the art object or expression itself, as opposed to the progressive, embodied, multimodal exploration of materials, objects, and tools by infants and very young children (cf. Deák, 2014, p. 154); which is not to say that children cannot engage in making art.

Taking this idea further to more complex and deep-rooted ways in which we make meaning and relate to art as makers, we can see how, compared to other common actions and activities such as using tools for purely instru-mental reasons or play-using tools as toys, the business of using tools to make art and to make art on its own seems different and, quite simply, pecu-liar. Making art is neither specifically instrumental nor play. Art making does not seem to have a distinct means-ends structure or underlying inten-tion, nor does it have a desire for make-believe or other similar complex pre-tense action (cf. Rakoczy et al., 2005; Austin, 1979). What is more, making art isn't only about pleasure, either. It is not right to assume that it is because making art affords us an avenue to experience the world through our inten-tional actions and our senses, that it is fundamental to our being in the world. Naturally, it is conceivable that experiencing the world through our actions and our senses, gives us pleasure (cf. McCarthy & Wright, pp. 68–69), and yes, it is human nature to seek pleasurable activities. But this line of thought doesn't link up with the scores of things we make as art or their diversity, or necessarily how we make them. There is a plenitude of examples of richly experiencing the world through our intentional actions and our senses, which most would agree have nothing in particular to do with making art; like roll-ing in mud, forest bathing, or eating viciously spicy food. The importance of making art is as much the pleasurable experience of the world, as the art as object is an expression of pure emotion (cf. Langer, 1941 [1976]).

This leads us to first reflect on the purpose of art and art processes and the motivation or desire that underlines making art. Following that, it leads us to question whether this purpose and motivation link up to the role of materials in making art. In other words, is somehow physically experiencing materials essential to the artmaking process? Ultimately, it also begs the question of why and how materials and the experience of making through them is important in this regard if they are not essential. Thus, bringing us, naturally, to question the place of digital space in terms of visual art.

Considering these questions in order to challenge the idea of the advanced, embodied, multimodal process of artmaking essentially linked to physical materials, we can look to Gedeon O. Deák, whose discussion about tools and the cognitive achievement that facilitates the use of tools informs our starting point. On the development of adaptive tool-use in early childhood and the sensorimotor, social, and conceptual factors that allow such use of tools, Deák ultimately asks why we develop an abstract concept of function of things at all (Deák, 2014, p. 170). Perhaps, he speculates, our ability to use tools and our abstract concept of function is a manifestation of something more fundamental, such as a general capacity for higher-order meta-conceptual reflection (Deák, 2014, p. 170). And perhaps, Deák continues in the same passage, this capacity is analogous with our capacity 'of metalinguistic conceptualization or reflection on high-order social structures (e.g., macroeconomics, political philosophy)'.

Perhaps it is. Nonetheless, making art is a comparable yet different human capacity. It is also something more. When we ask what art affords us, we are not merely interested in art as illustrations, representations, or depictions or an object as something to look at or handle. However useful those images most certainly are, they do little to engage us like art does. Rather, it seems more reasonable that through the contemplation of art objects and the art process itself, we are bringing to the fore other higher-order meta-conceptual reflections. More to the point, through art, we are conceptualising and reconceptualising the fullness of life and how we live it by including the imaginary, as it were, in reality while preserving its imaginary nature.

To widen our approach to art, we can consider the work of Alva Noë. Noë provides us with a discussion concerning the likes of the arts and philosophy and, through that discussion, a framework for understanding what art is and what it does. As such, Noë offers us not so much a justification as to why we make things, but rather an explanation for why we do so. Central to his discussion is that as human beings, we inherently strive to organise our being and action in the world. This organisational activity is a fundamental phenomenon of human life. First-order organisational activities of our being and action in the world are things like 'walking, talking, singing, thinking, making and deploying pictures for this task or that' (Noë, 2015, loc. 516). Taking note of this last activity, however, we find that pictures can serve many functions, and there is more to making things as art than just making and deploying pictures for different practical tasks. For example, a fast-food joint's pictures of the dishes on their menu are something other than a still-life painting, or even the Pop Art artist Claes Oldenburg's immensely over-sized soft sculpture, *Floor Burger (Giant Hamburger)* (1962). Art engages us at a deeper level, and as such not only helps us make sense of the world, it also allows us to reconceptualise what being in the world is like and what it can be like. We cannot freely choose to reconceptualise ourselves in the world like this; we must be prompted to do so. And art is such a stimulus that gives us the resources to reconceptualise ourselves in the world.

In this sense, making art is a second-order organisational activity; or, we could suggest through Deák, related to our capacity for higher-order meta-conceptual reflection. It is a human practice that puts our first-order organisation of ourselves on display for us, aiming to 'seek to bring out and exhibit, to disclose and to illuminate, aspects of the way we find ourselves organized' (Noë, 2015, loc. 286). Making things as art is, therefore, both an organisational and reorganisational practice, a duality that reflects the complexity of art and things as art in different types of media (e.g. Saethre-McGuirk, 2021). This duality is inherent to art, a characteristic of art, and, following this, is an essential aspect of art, too. Art completes its intricate errand of being an organisational and a reorganisational practice by what Noë refers to as looping (Noë, 2015, loc. 3788), by bringing to light our own organisation of our lives and simultaneously looping back and showing us the possibility of a different way of organising ourselves.

This seemingly lifts our understanding of art up and away from merely being about materials and physically handling materials to make things. Let it be clear: we make art and things as art because it is part of our human nature, and our ability to flexibly imagine, think, and understand through things facilitates and strengthens this process. Making art affords us new resources for thinking about how we organise ourselves, how we are disposed to organise ourselves, and how we could reorganise ourselves (Noë, 2015, loc. 3788). Art is an important practice for gaining a meta-perspective on our being in the world; making art and things as art makes us human, and the inverse of this is that we can make art because we are human. As a fundamental human practice, it is simultaneously a practice which is necessary for us to fulfil our potential as humans in the world (Noë, 2015, loc. 4014, loc. 4135). But exactly how it does this, so far at least, doesn't seem contingent upon materials and things we can touch. Indeed, artmaking processes can begin at an early age, and making art takes into service lots of materials that are beyond my physical grasp, like sound, light, and even smells.

This leads us to two important points. Firstly, we can speculate that the organisational and reorganisational practice of art and art processes are not something which is limited to adults. It is not that you have to have an established and mature view of yourself in the world to engage in the import of art or of making art. Childhood and youth are not incomplete forms of existence. On the contrary, since making things as art is a fundamental human activity that gives us insight into our being in the world, engaging with import or making things as art is an activity that benefits people of any age within their ability. It gives us the resources needed to reorganise ourselves in the world to the extent that we are able to and interested in doing so. Infants and very young children do this through their progressive, embodied, multimodule exploration of materials, objects, and tools. Continuously developing their abstract concept of function and understanding of affordances, they see, contemplate, and articulate through form and art, too. Rich materiality presents a wide range of characteristics that the young maker can explore. Having aesthetic experiences and developing their skills in this regard enables them to make more complex things as art. And secondly, while art is an intrinsic part of human life, it does not seemingly depend on materials. Therefore, we must ask how materials play into the art process in other ways, if indeed the presence and experience of physical things you can touch is nonetheless essential to art and art processes.

How materials play into art

Art affords us Noë's looping experience through our uniquely human capability to flexibly think and draw out an understanding of art's import, but it would seem that specifically how we chose to bring out and exhibit aspects of the way we find ourselves organised, what techniques, materials, or tools we use for this practice, is rather inconsequential for defining something as art or an artistic process. There are a number of art historical and contemporary practice examples which would prove that to be the case. At the same time, they are only part of the picture in relation to making things as art; indeed, the significance of materials has been underplayed in the discussion so far. We are missing the next link in our argument, relating to the physical experience of materials and the art process, flexible thinking, and even looping. In short, are materials and the physical experience of materials essential to how we can make things, as such an important aspect of human life available to ourselves and others?

Furthering this line of thought from the perspective of the viewer, we find that Nöe clearly holds that the experience of materials and the thing itself are essential for us to have that work of art make itself fully available to us. His argument seems completely reasonable. I would add that, if the arts are a fundamental human practice, making it possible to fulfil our potential in the world and necessitating this need for fulfilment, it does not make sense for us not to use or need all our senses and receptors to latch on to everything that art as things, actions, and events would offer us. Viewing art, I widen my experience of the work to include more than just what I can see. I 'see' it with a far more elaborate understanding of the work, including more than just the visual.

For Nöe, the materials of the thing seem to play a part in this intimate and communicative process I submit myself to as viewer (cf. Noë, 2015, loc. 1788, loc. 1883, loc. 2175, loc. 2484, loc. 3077); at one point, Noë bluntly states, 'Paintings are material and their materiality counts' (Noë, 2015, loc. 3066). I would tend to agree. The licked finish of Jacques-Louis David's *La Mort de Marat* (1793) does not hide the artist's hand as obviously, nor does Willem de Kooning's impastos radiate dynamism quite as forcefully when presented as a postcard, poster, or on a digital surface or a screen. However, the presence of materiality extends beyond the two-dimensional surface of the painting. Meret Oppenheim's *Object* (or *Le Déjeuner en fourrure)* (1936), a delicately fur-clad teacup, saucer, and spoon, does not quite lure forth the same strange mouthfeel sensation, accentuating its Surrealist underpinnings, when presented as a photograph. The work's transition from the real to the representational sphere is an articulative act, where the interface inevitably takes into service its own voice, from its own patterns of speech and linguistic landscape, so to speak (cf. Saethre-McGuirk, 2021). So, while the specific object or choice of materials in themselves is to a certain degree irrelevant, the physicality of art and its nature of being in the world for me as viewer is not. Especially when the alternative is meeting the work as a reproduction. When Noë claims that to perceive the thing is to see the whole thing in situ, he is also reacting against the idea that an image or a photograph of a work of art can have the same effect on us as the actual thing can (Noë, 2015, loc. 2484).

For the viewer, to see the thing is to perceive the whole thing in our shared space. Inherent in its form, and contingent upon the materials that make that form possible, art being in place and space bears import. Disregarding its scale and being in place and space – its installation – undermines the full nature of the work of art in addition to the representation of the materials themselves. For this reason, an image of a work of art cannot substitute the physical, in-person meeting with art. Donald Judd's minimalist stacks from the 1960s fully exemplify this. Geometric, seemingly identical and void of individual features, as well as ordered by strict principle, the forms nonetheless push to the fore the particular attributes of their whole while claiming space in relation to me as viewer. Their calm individual character becomes apparent to me as I make my acquaintance with the different works in the same series. Like members of a family, they are different from one another yet recognisably similar. In their stature before me, with their minute variations and obvious differences, I become even more aware of their distinct qualities. Following this, in that the shared physical experience of art is essential to experiencing something fully as art, the bearing of import in and of a work of art must be coupled with the materiality of the thing. In this way, the different arts and their materials take claim of our shared space, place, and time (cf. Langer, 1953). Translated in relation to the other arts, such as dance and literature, we can see how they use different forms and means to bear import; that is, present to us the possibility of looping back, embracing a higher-order meta-conceptual reflection.

So far, we recognise that art is an organisational and reorganisational practice and that the arts achieve this in different ways, through different means and materials. The viewer's offer of attention to the fullness of the object is complimented by the possibility of the object, in situ, completely occupying their senses in the space that they share. The promise of this interaction is made complete by the material presence of the object in its original form. While this is an important insight and good as far as it goes, Noë does not offer further insight into how experiences and materials play into making art, or into making and teaching the creative arts in the post-digital era. This position also leaves us with the conundrum of those works that are made digitally and exist fully in three-dimensional virtual space or even works that exist in augmented reality. Are these works not fully available to us, and how can we even make them, lacking as digital space is a multitude of things for our senses and receptors to latch on to?

Expanding our approach to this working proposal even more, then, we can get closer to the physicality of things – and hence the way materials and our experience of them are essential to art processes – by looking deeper into the inert creative potential of materials and objects. In other words, we need to see this relationship from the perspective of the maker. James J. Gibson, primarily known in the arts though his theory of affordances, proposes a way of viewing materials and objects as full of potential, which lends itself to the act of making art. His discussions about the affordances of materials as the objectively and physically possible action in relation to an object or environment are of special interest here, along with his work on perception.

Gibson formalised his definition of affordances of the environment as that which 'are what it offers the animal, what it provides or furnishes, either for good or ill' (Gibson, 1979, p. 127). Harry Heft, commenting on Gibson, noted that his idea of affordances has an underlying visual component; adding that it refers to the 'perceivable functional meanings of objects and events that are carried in the structure of ambient light' (Heft, 1989, p. 3). In this, Heft and Gibson reveal the close relationship between touch and sight, or haptic and visual information and knowledge about things. I would go even further. The way in which materials are available to the maker, the full extent to which they make themselves available to the maker, and the potential for a comprehensive poetic vocabulary of the materials, extends beyond the visual. The wealth of sensory information I collect about the world is not merely individually processed, compared to past experiences, sorted according to materials, and then archived. It is constantly at hand to me through all my senses, underlining the relational, dialectical dimensions of affordances when making things as art. When working with a material, I am in constant communication with the material, be it through touch, temperature or texture, pressure or resistance, or even sound or smell. We can draw some insight into the multifaceted experience of materials by borrowing Gibson's idea of human scale; meaning that the affordance of an event or object is seen in relation to the person who takes that affordance into use (cf. Heft, 1989, p. 3), not relational scale as in mere size or looming presence in a space. Rather, it is a relational quality paired with the maker, opening an understanding of the private experience of a wide range of sensory stimulus, the privacy of perception. Gibson held:

> Now I suggest that this state of affairs can define what might be called levels of increasing 'privacy' of perception. All observers can obtain exactly the same information about a tree if they all walk around it and get the same perspectives. Each observer gets a somewhat different set of perspectives of his own hands than any other observer gets, although there is much in common. But the perspective of one's own nose is absolutely unique and no one else can ever see it from that particular point of view. It is a completely private experience.
>
> (Gibson, 1967, p. 171)

Gibson seems to be saying that this privacy of perception has to do with the physical distance between the object and the perceptual uptake of it; seeing the tree outside of our body, feeling the tree against our body, or smelling the tree, literally, inside our body. Rather, I would argue that while the visual experience of the tree as more-public perception and the experience of the olfactory stimuli as more-private sensation are to a certain degree two different things in terms of physical distance to our points of perception, they are similar in that they concern how a person intimately makes sense out of the world. This idea of scale has to do with how someone sees and senses the world as something in relation to themselves: their individual body, senses, memories, and embodied knowledge combined.

Here, with regards to the scent of the tree, this borrowed idea has to do with how one perceives that scent, what one knows of it, and quite possibly what one personally associates with it. In an art process, the scent becomes a tool of sorts, which can be taken into service when conceptualising and formulating a meta-conceptual reflection, to be presented to the viewer for bringing to light the organisation of our lives and simultaneously looping back and showing us the possibility of a different way of organising ourselves. As such, viewers are not invited to smell the tree and widely ponder on the wildly different private experiences they may have of trees. Unless, of course, that is the specific import the maker was bringing to the fore through the work. Rather, the maker has taken in the smell of that tree or of trees into service, pared down their rich perception and knowledge of the tree to one or more components, aspects, or tools, and used that to articulate an import, which in turn may be interpreted in different but related ways. Indeed, in interpreting the work in different but related ways, the viewer is exercising the plasticity of the completed work and their flexible thinking about things, in effect in dialogue with the maker. In this, we can also see the role of the critic; auxiliary to the viewer's process of learning to 'lay hold of the full import of the work', the role of the critic is to design a space for the re-education of the viewer's perception of art (Dewey, 2005 [1934], pp. 299–300). To look past their experience of trees and see the forest, so to speak.

For the maker, affordances have both objective and subjective values. They reside in the overlapping space of interaction in between the maker and the materials. They happen within these boundaries, so do not belong to any which one alone – neither the person nor the material (Heft, 1989, p. 4) – and yet they are completely dependent on both. They are what the materials, object, or event offers the maker and others. They are also what the maker can see and sense in relation to their own body, and in particular how the maker uniquely understands the stimulus information that very material, object, or event offers. Affordances reflect the maker's aesthetic awareness of and attention to the world. Perceiving the world as predisposed of affordances 'simultaneously entails an awareness of both the environment and the body' (Heft, 1989, p. 12). As such, as Gibson claims, perceiving the world is particular type of awareness: 'It is a keeping-in-touch with the world, an experience of things rather than a having of experiences. It involves awareness-of instead of just awareness' (Gibson, 1979, p. 239).

In this, we can also sense the presence of Maurice Merleau-Ponty. The maker meeting the world through their body and their senses can be concerned with specific goal-directed actions 'with a directionality and an end implicit in their origins – in other word [*sic.*], intentional acts' (Heft, 1989, p. 11). Since intentional acts are always situated within the boundaries of interaction, a certain set of conditions are always inherent in an action. Thus, ultimately, one could suggest that the body itself in conjunction with the materials is the means for the individual's intentional repertoire to be expressed. This has implications for materials in relation to making things and art processes. Even though affordances organise, constrict, and facilitate the process of exploring, discovering, and intentionally interacting with the world, in an art process, things and materials do not have preordained possibilities of expression or form inherent in them; nor are there preordained possibilities of expression to be made available to the viewer. Inasmuch as the boundaries of interaction are set and, in many ways, dependant on the set of affordances made available because of the maker and the nature of the materials, the maker and the physical materials comprise an unambiguous ecology of an art process, which simultaneously affords a wide range of actions.

Makings and actions

Returning to our conundrum of making things in digital space as artistic space and experiencing those things in three-dimensional virtual or augmented space, it would seem that there are important differences to making in real space and in digital space. I argue, though, that while we might sometimes think of those differences as essential, they are not. Rounding off this chapter, I will address why the differences between real and digital artistic space are non-essential. In the following chapter, I discuss why they nonetheless can be experienced as essential.

By physically handling materials when making, I am not only directly connected to the materials; I experience myself as developing a more diverse, more encompassing embodied knowledge of them, too. Touching and handling materials while making allows me to experience the shape of a thing not just visually. It becomes space that is given form and that I can 'see' without vision; that is, by touch, smell, sound, and the like. My actions and my making in the real take full advantage of the connection I have with materials and form, and, importantly, how I see the object, both visually and otherwise. The task of immersing myself in this connection with materials and the possibility of expression, playing with artistic references, enables me to transform, develop, and present new ideas in the creative process, and then present them as form which others can reflect on (cf. Høffding & Snekkestad, p. 171, p. 172 & p. 174).

To better understand this task and to be able to later understand the pedagogical implications of it with regards to making in digital space, we can bring to the fore the free improvisation jazz saxophonist Torben Snekkestad's theoretical understanding of his performative acts, which he mapped out together with Simon Høffding (Høffding & Snekkestad, 2021, p. 167). With this starting point in relation to the act of making things, we can define the most basic level of making art as having the technical abilities to do so; that is, having the appropriate tools, techniques, stamina, and visual training, as well as having embodied knowledge about materials. When making, I must be able to see the possibility of an articulation of import in the materials, and I must be capable of intentionally acting through those materials. Seen as a whole, skills and the skilful use of tools is an important part of what it means to make art: Clearly, making art entails that I have to have skills and technical abilities in relation to materials, I have to be able to make use of my knowledge about those and other materials, and I have to have that knowledge close at hand while making.

It is important to note that tools do not invalidate my connection with my materials, which naturally come between me and my materials. Following the complex awareness of function (codified, instrumental tool use), affordances (multiple properties and potentials for interaction made visible to one), and skill (cf. Deák, 2014, pp. 153, 163), thinking through art processes promotes the negotiation of ways to use one's body. To compensate for difficult or different actions for particular purposes, any tool, as such, is an extension of the engaged body interacting with the potential of the materials at hand. A potential which is made visible to me through complex perceptual uptake and embodied knowledge (cf. Polanyi, 1969, p. 127). For this reason, my interaction with materials can be both direct and, through an extension of my body, indirect. The art process does not depend on the use of the body alone as the maker's advanced hands-on dialogue with the materials. I can intentionally and meaningfully act through a tool once I make that tool form a part of my own body through my experienced and skilled use of it. To Michael Polanyi, I am then aware of my body through the tool, in that I have interiorised the tool and made myself 'dwell' in it (Polanyi, 1969, p. 148). Polanyi explains:

> We may test the tool for its effectiveness or the probe for its suitability . . . but the tool and the probe can never lie in the field of these operations; they remain necessarily on our side of it, forming part of ourselves, the operating persons. We pour ourselves out into them and assimilate them as parts of our own existence. We accept them existentially by dwelling in them.
>
> (Polanyi, 1974, p. 59)

Before I dwell in the tool, before it extends my ability to perceive the materials at hand, it continues to uncomfortably rest between me and the materials.

As I learn to dwell in my tool, the divide between myself and the operation field, the materials, becomes less opaque. When working with paint on canvas, I concentrate on that which is becoming in artistic space, inside the canvas. My representational works can entail the forming of an imagined subject inside the three-dimensional space of artistic space, or on the other side of the flat canvas. When doing so, I build my form into that artistic space from an idea that is in the midst of being articulated, an imagined object so to speak, which is given as becoming to my mental gaze (cf. Casey, 1981, p. 146; cf. Langer, 1953, p. 78). I can sense the form in that space even before I give it form, and through that mental gaze, I can see the depth of the space, the curvatures of the objects therein, and my subject's presence. Only then does that space relate back to me through the surface's material characteristics, which in turn inform my gaze in a type of dialogue. More so than pouring myself into my tools, this internal imagery spreads out from my perception; through my hand and my particular grasp of the paintbrush, the paintbrush and the bend of its bristle, the paint that sits at the end of the individual bristle hairs and that coats, taints, or scratches the canvas, and through the canvas itself to the space inside the image. When I am in my tool, I work in that artistic space. This is in line with Merleau-Ponty, who commented that 'aesthetic perception . . . opens up a new spatiality, that the picture as a work of art is not in the space which it inhabits as a physical thing and as a coloured canvas' (Merleau-Ponty, 1962, p. 287). Indeed, artistic space is beyond that, and it is not confined to two-dimensional work on canvas.

My abstract works are no different in how they sit in artistic space as an articulated whole, although the urge for and consequently repulsion of the flatness of the canvas still lingers as an art historical backdrop to my actions in that space. For both representational and abstract work, though, I do not consistently dwell in my tool, be it paintbrush, paint, or canvas. Rather, the divide between me and my materials can be less or more opaque, which I am sure is a familiar experience to most pupils of art. Sometimes, I fully see the form as it is becoming in artistic space; seeing both artistic space and real space at once, as if with double sight, even though it is not a constant. As I become more familiar and skilled with the tool, I become more fully aware of both artistic space and real space, and I move more freely between the two. I lose sight of the artistic space within when the pearl of paint trapped at the tips of the bristle hairs fails to dissipate as I pull my paintbrush along the canvas. I change my grip and reposition my hand when I no longer can twist my arm to complete the line presented to me by my mental gaze. Sometimes without pause or notice, no doubt, other times in apparent frustration. In this, I switch from a situation-specific way of coping with my paintbrush to a detached rule-following way of holding my paintbrush, only to switch back again (cf. Dreyfus, 2005, p. 52). Surely dwelling fully and completely in one's tool and staying in artistic space is something primarily enjoyed by the most skilled amongst us. For the rest of us, the act of making includes taking being in, then out of artistic space into service.

Working in digital space as artistic space shares this relationship between me and my tools with real space as artistic space. Any difference is not an essential difference, even though it can be experienced as such, especially when I have insufficient mastery of my digital tools. There is, therefore, another, more fundamental reason why there is no essential difference between making in real, augmented, or digital space as artistic space. With regards to my knowledge about materials, my connection with those materials, and perceiving shape, as far as we have come in understanding the relationship between making art and materials, our discussion has concentrated on the here and now. That is, the immediate dialogue the maker has with materials or the tools while in the act of articulating import. That might be an oversimplification of the complex act of making art.

It seems unreasonable and unlikely that the intricacies of the act of making art only relates to past experience as the time it takes to make a piece or even become skilful with certain tools. Surely, making depends on bringing our other experiences and awareness of the world into the making act. Extending the act of making beyond the present reveals making's full and multifaceted nature in relation to the world. The child in the world has knowledge about the world and themselves in the world, and the articulate nature of the child in the world and the act of making art through being in the world is repeatedly and increasingly strengthened in an incremental fashion by the body directly precepting the world. It is not so much a hermeneutic circle as a hermeneutic spiral; a coherent and consistent process of physically interpreting materials through perceptions and linking knowledge and attitude of the world through processes of awareness-of, lending itself to a repeatedly and increasingly richer understanding of the boundaries of interaction (cf. O'Toole, 2018). Touching and handling things progressively advances our knowledge of the world and our ability to intentionally act in the world. Even the newly born will by mere reflex grasp a finger within its reach, but that action and experience also means something.

On the most basic level, for the progressiveness of the embodied and multimodal exploration of materials, objects, and tools by infants and very young children to be meaningful, it must either lead to some breakthrough event, a watershed moment leading to abstract concept of function, or in and of itself be cumulative, continuously and incrementally building upon previous perceptions and experiences. The latter seems a more reasonable process, and in either event, we must somehow bring with us and build on past experiences. Polanyi, in his essays on knowing and being (1969), says it well:

> Every time we make sense of the world, we rely on our tacit knowledge of impacts made by the world on our body and the complex responses

of our body to these impacts. Such is the exceptional position of our body in the universe.

(Polanyi, 1969, pp. 147–148)

In being in the world, we develop our personal knowledge of materials and tacit knowledge of acting on those materials, significantly and over time. 'All the music you've ever heard in your life is somewhere in your head', Snekkestad claimed (Høffding & Snekkestad, 2021, p. 172). Similarly, all of the forms and all of the materials you have ever worked with are in your head and in your hands. Specific and general past experiences and responses come into play while perceiving materials and recognising their particular affordances, as well as when contrasting affordance or acknowledging a lack of affordances. We can appreciate this thought when considering how it is to work with a versatile material, such as clay. From mud cakes to pinch pots, and later to building slab structures and throwing vases, I have culti-vated my ability for intentional acts in clay through my past experiences, my cumulative insight into the different types of clay and other pliable, soft materials, and my immediate experience with the material at hand. Those just-past and long-past comprehensive experiences and insights are brought into my making in the now, both informing my unconscious and intentional handling of and interaction with the material. This tacit knowledge creates its own ambience, feeding into a realm of possible future action in at least two different but connected ways.

First, to understand how this ambience comes into play in making pro-cesses, I can reflect back on early memories of digging in and playing with the clay-laden earth of my childhood. Asked now, I can recall sporadic memories of casting mud cakes on wooden benches and having them col-lectively bake to a crisp under the hot summer sun. Memories of the satis-faction of being able to pry the flat form off its surface without breaking it and being able to see and run my fingers over the rich landscape of veins on its underbelly are not without value. But such memories are more a personal narrative than a concrete, mnemonic exercise or tool. Working with ceram-ics, I do not draw on those experiences in some romanticising moment of personal reflection. Rather, I could draw on unspoken, tacit knowledge about materials and my action with it: This is when it breaks. This is when the veins crumble. Or my insight into form: This is what the visual shape of the vein feels like. This is the top of the curvature of a balanced shape. Based on similar experience, I know how moist clay needs to be for me to be able to form it and when it is too moist to hold a shape. I also know how dry it needs to be for me to be able to smooth rough edges off of it before loading it in the kiln for firing. I know its shape, and to a certain degree, what it will be like after shrinking in the kiln.

It is sometimes relatively easy to judge, when I am not actively shaping it or in the act of making, and the thing itself is rather stationary. Looking at it, the surface reveals visual clues. I can hold it against my cheek to feel its temperature and check its moisture, and smell it, even. I take my time with the thing, piecing together the different inputs and making a judgement that I can test out, question, and change. I call on my tacit knowledge of the materials or the thing at hand when handling it, as well as take the thing in with all of my senses. This puts Gibson's tree observer's public perceptions and private sensations into perspective. We may obtain exactly the same perception information about a tree when walking around it or maybe even from touching it, but my private experience of smelling it is not separated from this public percept. Rather, for me the visual, tactile, and olfactory experiences come together as I experience the tree; the experience as a whole is absolutely unique, in effect a completely private experience. It is within this private experience that I have a repertoire of intentional acts, situated within the boundaries of interaction. Without my experience of the past, the range of the affordances of the materials and making in artistic space in the now is reduced.

Second, it is different when I am in the act of making or actively giving form to the materials. For the most part, it usually goes much faster. At times, I need to be able to read all of the input nearly simultaneously. But what is more, I soon find myself calling on a different kind of insight into the materials. It is a mature, advanced multimodal insight, which is more than being able to absorb a quicker succession of input. It is experiencing the input as a conglomerated whole and moving forward past that moment of perception: It is all one and the same perception. The placement of my hand, the resistance to my touch, and the sound of the object, combined, change the course of what is possible. This insight is a far more intimate insight into the act of making that is more difficult to acquire and strenuous to consciously to call on. This type of knowledge combines the ambience of knowing and the act of doing. Polanyi partially but inadequately articulates this knowledge of knowing and being in relation to medical expertise: 'To percuss a lung is as much a muscular feat as a delicate discrimination of the sounds thus elicited. The palpation of a spleen or a kidney combines a skilful kneading of the region with a trained sense for the peculiar feeling of the organ's resistance' (Polanyi, 1969, p. 126).

This tacit knowledge – both simple and complex – is knowledge about my materials, but also about me interacting with materials. That is not to say that I must have extensive experience with every imaginable material, forms of that material, and variations in a material or a type of space to be able to make things. My ambient tacit knowledge of materials and other general types of materials is useful when making and especially when making something new, because no two lumps of clay can ever be exactly the same, just as no pieces of wood or blocks of marble can ever truly be replicated. I go into making things, working with materials, and making in different spaces knowing that I am always doing something different from what I have done before, and so, I can project my knowledge of a material or a space into seeing possibilities of making with new or even different materials. My same-as-but-different experience of other particular materials and objects can come into play as scaffolding, leading to new insight when working with materials otherwise unknown to me, such as digital materials. For this reason, I can possibly draw on my digital drawing surface and appreciate the softness of its unique line because I have used soft pencils before. In this complex articulate act, I can take knowledge about materials and space and scaffold that insight onto working with new materials and under new conditions, when working with them. Therefore, my ambient experiences are essential as they enable my process of making things, no matter which materials I work with or what space I work in. I become better able to position myself and my work in digital space as artistic space when I have a wide range of real experiences to draw on.

These examples illustrate how I bring the past with me as I move forward in the creative act, the importance of a rich experience of and awareness of the world, of being in contact with materials, and being able to see the thing, as it were, in the full and with all of my senses. This is the fundamental reason that there is no essential difference between making in the different forms of artistic space. Some of these accumulated embodied and multimodal experiences and responses of the past may come into play in the act of making as physical skills; muscular acts in the now that also link up to that moment of making just beyond the now. However, such muscular acts are more than mere knee-jerk reactions, such as pulling away from an expected shock (cf. Polanyi, 1983, p. 8). In this sense, they are more like a fine-tuned coordinative first-order organisational act or activity, like walking, bicycling, or swimming. Perhaps taking advantage of my physical skills in my mature, multimodal insight into making is like an absorbed coping, a reckoning with the actual materials at hand; such as with staying afloat when, suddenly or not, finding myself in deep water, and where my floating action is an immediate response to my surroundings (cf. Romdenh-Romluc, 2011, p. 93). In such a case, it is my actual surroundings (the water), task (not drowning), and motor skills (floating) that determine my bodily movements. Tasked with not drowning in deep water, I stay afloat. Likewise, I do not put any special thought into how to use a pencil when drawing or how to form a shape in three-dimensional digital space.

These actions require employing those motor skills which are seen as relevant to the environment and task at hand: 'It is the agent's *actual* environment and the project in which she is *actually* engaged – together with her motor-skills – that shape the content of her perceptions, which initiate and control absorbed coping' (Romdenh-Romluc, 2007, p. 51). There is clearly something of this in making art. In Komarine Romdenh-Romluc's (2011) reading of Merleau-Ponty, she exemplifies reckoning with the actual through the piano player: 'The presence of a piano, and the project of playing it . . . make the pianist's ability to play available to them so that they can both perceive the piano as playable and actually play it' (Romdenh-Romluc, 2011, p. 94). I would expand on this. So close is the musician's relationship between perceiving the instrument as playable and actually playing it that an affliction such as forms of musician's dystonia, a task-specific neurological movement disorder, while painless, is highly disabling (Altenmüller & Jabusch, 2010, p. 31), in addition to the anxiety associated with the imperfect playing that follows musician's dystonia possibly being 'too disabling for the musician's career to continue' (Sussman, 2015, p. 318).

While contending with the actual is important, as a whole, making art is dependent on more than just mastering skills. This leads us to two insights. First, reckoning with the actual is present in working with materials. For example, working with silver, I cannot create a reticulated and rippled textured surface without tacit knowledge of to what length the hand is extended by the heat of the torch, how the material is heated over its surface, when the rippling is about to commence, and when and how much the torch needs to be pulled back to slow down and stop the process at hand. These skills are comparable to the pianist perceiving the piano as playable and then actually playing it. But secondly, I engage in artmaking in a different manner than how I merely draw with a pencil, or for that matter, play a piano or any other instrument or work with silver. There is more to making in an art process than merely recognising that wet clay is soft and cold silver is hard and knowing what to do with it. The moment to come, that split second when I have internalised the sensory information available to me while in the act of making, leading to that moment before a new act takes place, is in this sense both actual and possible. Reckoning with the possible encompasses 'possible projects that the agent could undertake, and/or possible environments in which she could be located' (Romdenh-Romluc, 2007, p. 51). I can see these possibilities for intentional acts because of an array of past experiences, both specific and general, which are part of this ambience of making. In working with materials with the purpose of making art, I need to able to pick up on not one opportunity for action, but many opportunities for action; I need to be able to look past the thing-as-for-action and rather think of the actions-possible-through-the-thing (cf. Romdenh-Romluc, 2007, pp. 45–46). Back to our floating example of reckoning with the actual, we are not interested in floating-as-for-not-drowning, but rather ways-to-keep-breathing. This is at once projecting a situation around myself and summoning invitations to act on the world; it is not merely summoning invitations to behave from the world (cf. Romdenh-Romluc, 2007).

So, more than just playing the piano, making art could be compared to being a pianist practicing musical improvisation, or being able to play and improvise beyond that which is immediately available to me. So, while motor skills as physical abilities and capacities in relation to working with materials naturally underpin art making, art making as a whole isn't covered by that alone. I can, but do not have to, stick to the conventional way of working with a material when making art. I can find impetus to articulate my import differently through working with different materials because they force me to think inside the constraints that they offer. One could argue, even, that this is a core value of art and art education (e.g. Eisner, 2002, pp. 236–238). The flexible thinking of an art process enables me to think differently about how to engage the materials; at the same time I must be sufficiently aware of my tools and my materials in an advanced multimodal manner. I improvise on the basis of my past experiences of form, materials, and making. Within the relational boundaries of action between maker and materials, my ambient experiences follow me as maker and present themselves as at once both the basis for the perceived affordance and that which extends itself beyond that affordance alone. This leads to the understanding that physical experiences play into the flexible thinking of things, seeing of things, and making things, as making art starts with my gaze and my knowledge of materials and the world, not the artistic space itself – real or digital. This, as we will see, is important for teaching, and especially so in relation to digital space.

Bibliography

Altenmüller, E., & Jabusch, H.C. (2010). Focal dystonia in musicians: Phenomenology, pathophysiology and triggering factors. *European Journal of Neurology, Special Issue: Dystonia, 17*(1), 31–36.

Austin, J.L. (1979). Pretending. In J.O. Urmson & G.J. Warnock (Eds.), *Philosophical papers*. Oxford University Press.

Casey, E.S. (1981). Sartre on imagination. In P.A. Schilpp (Ed.), *The philosophy of Jean-Paul Sartre*. Open Court.

Deák, G.O. (2006, May 31–June 3). *Representing object functions: The cognitive basis of tool-use by children* [conference paper], Fifth International Conference on Development and Learning (ICDL'06), Indiana University.

Deák, G.O. (2014). Development of adaptive tool-use in early childhood: Sensorimotor, social, and conceptual factors. *Advances in Child Development and Behavior, J. B. Benson, 46*, 149–181.

Dennett, D.C. (1987). *The intentional stance*. MIT Press.

Dewey, J. (2005 [1934]). *Art as experience*. Penguin Publishing Group.

Dreyfus, H.L. (2005). Overcoming the myth of the mental: How philosophers can profit from the phenomenology of everyday expertise. *Proceedings and Addresses of the American Philosophical Association, 79*(2), 47–65.

Eisner, E.W. (2002). *The arts and the creation of mind*. Yale University Press.

Gibson, J.J. (1967). New reasons for realism. *Synthese, 17*(2), 162–172.

Gibson, J.J. (1979). *The ecological approach to visual perception*. Houghton-Mifflin.

Heft, H. (1989). Affordances and the body: An intentional analysis of Gibson's ecological approach to visual perception. *Journal for the Theory of Social Behaviour, 9*(1), 1–30.

Høffding, S., & Snekkestad, T. (2021). Inner and outer ears: Enacting agential systems in music improvisation. In S. Ravn, S. Høffding, & J. McGuirk (Eds.), *The philosophy of improvisation: Interdisciplinary perspectives on theory and practice*. Routledge.

Kahnweiler, D.H. (1949). *The sculptures of Picasso* (A.D.B. Sylvester, Trans.). Rodney Phillips.

Langer, S. (1941 [1976]). *Philosophy in a new key: A study in the symbolism of reason, rite and art*. Harvard University Press.

Langer, S. (1953). *Feeling and form: A theory of art*. Scribner.

McCarthy, J., & Wright, P. (2004). *Technology as experience*. MIT Press.

Merleau-Ponty, M. (1962 [2014]). *Phenomenology of perception* (D. Landes, Trans.). Routledge.

Noë, A. (2015). *Strange tools: Art and human nature* (Kindle ed.). Hill and Wang.

O'Toole, M. (2018). *The Hermeneutic Spiral and Interpretation in Literature and the Visual Arts*, Routledge.

Penrose, R. (1981). *Picasso: His life and work* (3rd ed.). University of California Press.

Polanyi, M. (1958 [1974]). *Personal knowledge: Towards a post-critical philosophy*. University of Chicago Press.

Polanyi, M. (1969). *Knowing and being*. University of Chicago Press.

Polanyi, M. (1983). *The tacit dimension*. Peter Smith.

Rakoczy, H., Tomasello, M., & Striano, T. (2005). On tools and toys: How children learn to act on and pretend with 'virgin objects'. *Developmental Science, 8*(1), 57–73.

Romdenh-Romluc, K. (2007). Merleau-Ponty and the power to reckon with the possible. In T. Baldwin (Ed.), *Reading Merleau-Ponty: On phenomenology of perception*. Routledge.

Romdenh-Romluc, K. (2011). *Merleau-Ponty and phenomenology of perception*. Routledge.

Saethre-McGuirk, E.M. (2021). An i for an eye: The collective shaping of experience in the age of machine-mediated art. In M. La Caze & T. Nannicelli (Eds.), *Truth in visual media: Aesthetics, ethics and politics*. Edinburgh University Press.

Sussman, J. (2015) Musician's dystonia. *Practical Neurology, 15*(4), 317–322. https://doi.org/10.1136/practneurol-2015-001148

3 Understanding making art in digital space as artistic space

Experiencing digital space as different

From our very beginning and through the exploration of objects, tools, and materials, we increasingly become aware of the world by advancing and intensifying our perception of the world around us. Our awareness of the world is taken into service in art processes through different avenues. It enables our articulation of import in relation to materials and making things, at whatever level that articulation may be. It enables the use of different materials, processes, and techniques. And it enables us to scaffold an awareness of one material or tool to another. By constantly honing my skills with materials and tools, I simultaneously experience a dwelling in my tools at different intensities. My emerging material knowledge and tools skills cultivate to an ever-greater degree my ability to see the possibilities for action and to stay in my tools and artistic space. Being fully at ease with making presupposes that I can expand my understanding of the possible beyond the here and now and keep my presence in the artistic space just before me, including in digital space.

In this way, my accumulative awareness of being in the world and insight into the physicality of things is important for things to show up to me in the post-digital era; in viewing art, by perceiving the whole thing in our shared space, place, and time, and in making art, through being aesthetically aware of the world and through handling real materials. When seeing and feeling the materials in my hands or through my tools, when giving form to import and communicating through the materials in the act of making, even wider boundaries of interaction are opened up to me and I can further act on and through those materials. I do not just feel materials and their qualities: I see, smell, and hear them, too, and I am made aware of and address these qualities through both my hands and my tools. Dependent on more than just tool skills alone, art processes entail that I can use specific and past experiences and awareness of the world when making art. Understanding this elucidates

DOI: 10.4324/9780429326264-3

the importance of materials and the role that they play in making things and teaching the creative arts in the post-digital era.

With this backdrop in place, even though the differences between working in the different artistic spaces are non-essential to the art process, it seems clear that I nonetheless experience there to be important differences. Making in digital space offers particular characteristics to the making process and to teaching the creative arts in the post-digital era, where making in and outside of digital space fluidly overlaps. It is at times a space seemingly like none other I can relate to in terms of making. The question is, then, in what way is making in digital space experienced as different from making in real space, especially when they overlap this way?

No longer consigned to the real alone, in the post-digital era artmaking happens in a fluid, real to augmented to digital field, rather indifferent to any imagined cordoning off of where and when things can be made, as well as how things can be made as art. This artmaking is not reactionary, as in necessarily anti-analogue, and it embraces a technological use-non-use approach while knowing that making in digital space is not seamlessly the same as making in real space. It can be experienced as essentially different, even though it is not. But to ignore its differences would be to not take digital space seriously as a space for making art.

With this in mind, there are many different avenues to approach making in digital space and the experience of digital space as artistic space. From an art historical perspective, we could start with early works such as Nam June Paik's video art, where cellist Charlotte Moorman's strangely melodic 1976 performance of Paik's appropriately titled *TV cello* (1971) has been made available to us today, ironically, on YouTube (AGNSW, 2011). We could then leap forward 50 years to contemporary work by artists such as Fiona Hillary, whose situated practice piece *Reverberating Futures* (2021) at Mission to Seafarers in Melbourne, Australia, takes into service virtual reality to articulate to her public the Siren-like beauty of the bioluminescent glow of climate change-nourished algae. The fullness of that piece depends on using virtual reality as a tool to position viewers at a central beachside site, and Hillary does this without breaking her stride in formulating and presenting the piece. While some contemporary works, such as Hillary's, include digital spaces and tools in the piece as it is performed, other works aim to articulate the digitalness of modern-day society or engage directly with hardware and software, putting digital tools and programmes at the centre of the import of the piece.

While such an art historical account of digital art – that is, all that is made fully or partially in digital space or remotely digitally enhanced (cf. Paul, 2016) – is interesting and relevant, it is not our main concern. We are less interested in works that comment on or take into service digital tools and new media in their own right, in this study of making art in digital space. We are more interested in the making process itself; the experience of digital space in giving form to something and the articulation of artistic import as objects. Because of this, it is necessary for us to pare down the plethora of different ways in which digital space can show up in relation to making art in particular. That is, in the two-dimensional and three-dimensional spaces which may be virtual or augmented, where that which is given as becoming to the maker's mental gaze is, in this process, given form through the use of digital tools or interfaces. In particular, we are interested in looking at the maker's intuitive range of actions, as those actions spread into digital space in the act of making.

Nonetheless, our concern is undoubtedly with art and not, as it were, the making of just anything digitally. At first glance, it does seem unreasonable that the intention of artmaking in and of itself constitutes an essentialness of what it means to make art. Surely one could argue that, apart from my concern with the accurateness of positioning my hand within the three-dimensional space or two-dimensional plane while painting, for example, the actual movements associated with art painting differ little from the instrumental painting-of-something to cover it with paint. Likewise, on a practical level, it seems difficult to differentiate between sculpting in a virtual space and merely giving form to a practical object in that space. In both sculpting examples, the maker can be wholly conducting their actions in digital space, and quite possibly never physically touch their objects until those objects are transitioned into the real.

However, as we have seen through our discussion concerning the creative arts and art processes, there is an important difference between the two. I continue to hold that the organisational and reorganisational practice constitutes an essential difference between making art and other making processes; this is also so in digital space. The practice of artmaking begins as a higher-order meta-conceptual reflection, and it is articulated in and through my mental gaze as I work it into a final import through continuous interaction with the material in an artistic space. The dialectics of invoking something meaningful by giving form to it is a journey between my mental gaze and the artistic space. This dialectical process is naturally also the basis for working in the digital sphere. Because of this, I do not conceive a complete and finished piece in my head, making my only struggle that of giving digital form to it through tools and materials outside of my body that only exist in digital space. As we will explore in this chapter, the understanding that this dialectical process is part and parcel of making in any space affords us the opportunity to uncover characteristics of digital space and to identify why that space can be experienced as different from real space.

Embodied space

To make sense of artmaking in digital space as a dialectical process through interaction with digital materials, I must examine this digital space in full. Note, however, that when I use the term 'the digital space' or 'digital materials', I do not merely mean virtual reality or representations of space or materials, like a digital replica of physical materials or a physical room. Rather, I use the terms 'digital space and materials' to cover what both the tool and system as digital interfaces present to me.

The tool itself exists as a physical barrier and an interface in the most practical, hands-on sense of the term. As such an interface, devices like my camera, drawing surface, or VR set enable me to make things in the digital field. Those interfaces carry with them technical idiosyncrasies that leave their own mark on whatever I make with them. For example, my camera can't catch the light the same way my eye does because it cannot pick up on all of the shades of grey or colour that I can, nor the angle of view of my vision (Saethre-McGuirk, 2021). My drawing surface can't render the silver shine of my pencil line or the absorbent black of my charcoal smudge, because the line lays behind the interface and when I look at my line on the device surface, it is not the line I am looking at but the glass surface of the device (Saethre-McGuirk, 2022). These are technical peculiarities of the physical tool as interface.

Furthermore, the interface can also be an experienced barrier that you cannot literally touch or hold on to. For our purposes, the system – that is, the software or programme that I use for making – is also a formidable interface. In and of itself, the software or programme can be my subject, for example in unpacking the cultural assumptions which lay underneath artificial intelligence or otherwise engaging directly with the programme at hand, but it is more often than not simply my tool for making. The software also carries its own technical characteristics or identities, sometimes reinforcing the mark of the physical technology and other times making that mark more complex, multifaceted, and difficult to identify. Traits, attributes, and qualities can as easily belong to any one device or system, and more often than not it seems, both (Saethre-McGuirk, 2021). For example, an application can frame my work in a particular fashion and a programme can shroud an area or angle, which I cannot see past no matter how much I move my body. Also, the nature of the system is such that the force of my actions on the physical barrier are on their own of no real consequence. Years of aggressively prodding digital surfaces with my fingertip when they fail to react to me testify to that. It is the device and the system, not only my own actions, which determine the aesthetic qualities of the line made or the object given form.

Together, these gadgets and interfaces afford me the means for making something; not just building blocks, lines, and shapes, but space, too. A space that does not exist in the real, but that is nonetheless experienced: digital space. Borrowing from Merleau-Ponty the insight that 'Space is not the setting (real or logical) in which things are arranged, but the means whereby the positing of things becomes possible' (Merleau-Ponty, 1962 [2012], p. 243), we see that digital space is the means, the tool, the materials, and the setting, independently but also combined, where the positing of these things is possible. Moving forward, it is unnatural to distinguish between digital and analogue space in that it is all artistic space, but I argue that it is necessary to do just that for the purpose of this study.

Digital space stems from the device and the system and can be understood to share the complex identity of both. Digital space can thus be an artistic space comparable to the physical surface of a piece of paper or a canvas unique to artmaking (cf. Merleau-Ponty, 1962 [2012], p. 287). As such an artistic space, two-dimensional digital space as a space for making does not differ greatly from that in the real, even though the nature of two-dimensional digital space can amplify one's perception of the space's qualities. On the one hand, digital space can be unapologetically flat. Triumphantly flat, even. That digital space is quite possibly more flat than what the art critic Clement Greenberg could ever have hoped for in his favoured mid-century American abstract painting (cf. Schreyach, 2015). Its flatness is intrinsic to its form and intensified by the characteristics of the digital as tool. On the other hand, this two-dimensional digital space can also be endlessly deep, engulfing the maker and viewer alike in its fractal-like depth. And likewise, paradoxically, the abyss of the space behind the interface is also intrinsic to it as tool and system. While potentially much deeper, this space, too, is similar to that of making in the real.

Things become increasingly interesting when we look into the experience of digital space beyond the two-dimensional surface of the device and system and the space therein. That is, the three-dimensional space which exists solely because of the device and system as interfaces, such as with virtual reality, and that real and virtual space which plays off of reality in different ways, such as with augmented reality. That range of reality between the real and the virtual is in this regard all digital space to some extent, in that my experiences in that diverse range are never fully released from the real nor fully immersed in the virtual, unless of course that space is first, foremost, and only real. This full range of digital space can be made available to me as artistic space. Then, both the real and the virtual are like onstage backdrops that appear at different distances from me while active in this space. I could engage through the characteristics of digital space in purposely and actively staying in digital space during my making process and keeping my awareness of real space at bay, staying in the flow of making in digital space. It is tempting since digital space allows my creative process to expand in ways which are otherwise difficult, impractical, or otherwise unrealistic. In obsessing over the objects I make while making them, digital space can allow me to study them in detail, in minutiae, in otherwise unfeasible ways. Likewise, large objects that are impossible to see in one whole can be shrunk, turned, flipped, and handled. Even if I have no intention of bringing that which was made in digital space into the real, I can immerse myself into my object in this way, as I actively alter my ability to see the thing at hand while modifying its relational qualities to me.

It might be tempting to stay in that digital space, but it is not practical. Giving form to an object in virtual reality that then exists in that world, and when my intention is eventually to bring it into the real, I must nonetheless be aware of the object as it will exist in the real and how the object as import will show up to others in the real. I can form it, move it, turn it, lift it, but my attention is also on how it will sit in real space and how it will visually relate to those around it once in the real; in short, its presence in situ. Imagining that presence is at times so clear that I see it in digital space as in situ. Other times, I am not convinced by my perception of it, and I have to strain to see the thing in real space. Failing that, the need to share real space with the thing stems from my unsatisfactory perceptual connection with the possibility of the digital space object to be in situ. I often also want to touch it and not just take it in with my eyes, so that I can more fully connect with the shape of it, the feel of it, and the make of it in relation to myself and others. However, while I understand why this is important, it concerns my action in that space more so than my understanding of that space and embodiment.

What is more, though, I have to stay aware of both backdrops of space when making for other practical reasons. Until someone actually invents Star Trek's holodeck or the omnidirectional treadmills and heat-sensitive haptic suits in Ready Player One (2018), these practical issues will remain. As a maker in virtual three-dimensional space, I am positioned in the real while the programme defines my boundaries and prevents me from hurting myself or those around me, for example by accidentally walking into a wall or hitting someone by what can been seen by those outside of my digital space as flailing arms and erratic gestures when I am making things in virtual reality. This leads me to share a strange relationship with those outside my digital space. At first in a room with others, though I don my virtual reality equipment and enter into the space, I am alone unless we are there together. I hear those outside of the digital space share in my experience, but I don't quite connect with them. Not unlike Merleau-Ponty's schizophrenic, who can hear a bird that is twittering in the garden, and who knows that there is a bird and that it is twittering but who only sees the gulf between them, 'as if the bird and the twittering had nothing to do with each other' (Merleau-Ponty, 1962 [2012], p. 282). Although I at times forget about the others around me in real space, I am still in the space we share, I still feel the same ground, and the real space remains structured for me. Yet, that which takes place in digital space feels as real as that in real space: So intertwined can digital and real space be at times that I act and react as if I was in the real.

This braiding together of experienced space can also be taken advantage of when experiencing what I make. Not only do programmes build boundaries into our experience of being in that space, but some programmes even take advantage of those boundaries, making the virtualness of the programme less obvious, becoming more like augmented virtual reality in form. For example, I can visit an exhibition of a virtual architectural space by exploring a physical structure that mirrors the virtual room I see through virtual reality equipment. This was the case at the architectural exhibition at the National Museum in Oslo, Norway (2018), whose title could be translated as 'The Forest in the House: An exploration of parallel realities'. Walking around in the virtual space that was visually and auditorily augmented by the real, the experience of my presence in that virtual space was strengthened. In that case, the floors and stairs I ascended and descended and the sounds of my steps all fed into the virtual world I experienced. At the other end of the continuum, I can imagine a piece which virtually takes its place in the real space that I share with others, but which is only visible to me when wearing the right equipment. In that augmented space, any objects I place there are like illusions that I can manipulate and work with at will, but that only I can see in interaction with the real things around it. Like a lie hidden between two truths, these virtual but real spaces can be experienced as the most real space of them all.

These examples of how digital space appears demonstrate how it in many ways can be experienced as real and digital space braided together. When experienced as one and – nearly – the same, the differences that do show up to me feel all the more prominent, essential even. While they are non-essential, they can irritate and seem important. Having examined the framework of digital space, I now must come to terms with how I can experience it as different. As my body is always physically on the outside of digital space, we can start off by comparing digital space to how the theatre stage shows up to us, where we immerse ourselves in the plot's imagined history. However, we rarely actively partake in the unfolding of the story and its ending; neither do we find ourselves as figures of action in the world of the stage. Rather, we sit as observers outside the world of the stage, as if peeping through some forcefield to the other side. Clearly, this doesn't correspond with how we experience three-dimensional digital space, where my experience is much more immediate.

In her note on film, Susanne Langer was closer to an understanding of space that, in contrast to the space of theatre, attends to this immediacy. On its mode of showing up to the viewer, Langer expounded:

> This is, essentially, *the dream mode*. I do not mean that it copies dream, or puts one into a daydream. Not at all; no more than literature invokes memory, or makes us believe that *we* are remembering. . . . Cinema is 'like' dream in the mode of its presentation: it creates a virtual present, an order of direct apparition.
>
> (Langer, 1953, p. 412)

She continues:

> The most noteworthy formal characteristic of dream . . . is that the dreamer is always at the center of it. Places shift, persons act and speak, or change and fade – facts emerge, situations grow, objects come into view with strange importance, ordinary things infinitely valuable or horrible, and they may be superseded by others that are related to them essentially by feeling, not by natural proximity. But the dreamer is always 'there', his relation is, so to speak, equidistant from all events. Things may occur around him or unroll before his eyes; he may act or want to act, or suffer or contemplate; but the *immediacy* of everything in a dream is the same for him.
>
> (Langer, 1953, p. 413)

How one perceives film space as intimate is comparable to how I experience digital space, in that digital space creates a virtual present, an order of direct apparition. I am not peeping through something to somewhere; rather, I am virtually there. Yet, digital space does not fully show up to me as cinematic space because in the act of making, things and places do not exist simply because of someone else's eventful storyline. My agency is governed by the system or programme, which determines where I can go, what I can do, as well as what I can experience once I am doing something where I am. But I am still free to roam and visit this space on terms that are somewhat my own. For me in the act of making, the raison d'être of the space is to give me as much freedom for making as possible, and, as opposed to film specifically, the things that happen in digital space and the objects that I make there do not merely seem like my own creation, my direct experience, and my reality (cf. Langer, 1953, p. 414); they are mine.

In this sense, the way that digital space shows up to me when making is similar to the gaming experience. It's differences in relation to theatre and film are small but significant. In their particular ways, theatre and film both strive to hold on to the viewer's attention, much like how in traditional gaming the aim is to hold the player completely present in the gaming space. And, like theatre and film space, traditional gaming simultaneously works hard to push the player's awareness of the real world into the background, thus holding them in the virtual world (Keogh, 2018, p. 74). Where theatre and film presents a world to the audience that only seems like one's own sensory experience (Langer, 1953, p. 414), gaming space holds on to its players by being a space of action and agency. Indeed, more like gamers who 'do not simply step into the virtual worlds of videogames but instead actively construct virtual worlds through engaging with the particular images, sounds, and devices of different videogames' (Keogh, 2018, p. 74), visitors in digital space can and must actively engage with the particularities of that digital space to keep their presence there all the more focused; not through a gaming story line, but through being there or even being in the flow of making. This is especially true when I am making in digital space without the intention of bringing the thing made into the real. The things I make then have a digital life, so to speak, and completely exist in digital space. Not only do I want to stay in that space and actively engage with my things, but my things will never have to leave that space, either.

When making in digital space something which will someday exist in the real, though, there are more than just practicalities (such as not hitting myself) that divide my awareness of space. I am also interested in keeping an awareness of both worlds while making for art process reasons. I position myself intentionally both in the virtual and the real in these cases. As such, my experience of digital space is similar to Brendan Keogh's particular game space where the player is co-attentive, positioned and balancing between the real and the game space (Keogh, 2018, p. 73). Keogh's co-attentive player never fully forgets that they exist in the actual world; their sense of immersion is shared between the two fields and they are 'paradoxically fully attentive to both worlds at the same time,' Keogh states, continuing, 'This is less a division of attention and more an amalgam of attentions' (Keogh, 2018, p. 72). For Keogh, the co-attentive player is aware of the tool as interface while in the act of playing and cannot or does not want to completely immerse themselves in the game. For our maker who might worry about accidentally damaging expensive gear, co-attentiveness is useful. For our maker who makes with the intention of bringing the object into the real, complete immersion would be counterproductive. For them, just as with Keogh's particular game space players, the space fulfils its function (cf. Keogh, 2018, p. 73) when both spaces are present.

The idea of co-attentive presence in digital space supports how I figure myself in digital space when making. As opposed to the possibilities for mobility and action in traditional immersive game space, co-attentive presence does not undermine my sensed and experienced presence in real space. I would be too far away from giving form to the thing if I had to work as immersed or through an avatar (cf. Crick, 2011, p. 264). Making something through an avatar seems as such awkward: I have no need to be represented in digital space by a being that is native to that space, because it undermines my experience of my body in the artistic space in full, of materials and making in digital space as artistic space. It would only be with great difficulty that I could, even if I wanted to, leave behind my embodied knowledge of movement and the fleshy presence of my body when making in digital space (cf. Crick, 2011, p. 265), because it is through my one body that I can experience artistic space expanded in this way when giving form to things. And so, no bird's-eye view nor avatar's movements can more directly connect me to my field of action (cf. Crick, 2011, p. 266), because my body and my experiences are central to my work there, too. Only a lack of habitual familiarity with my digital implements and interfaces would frustrate my dwelling in my tools or in this space. When I am fully familiar with my tools in relation to the materials there, I experience co-attentiveness in this space without my direct awareness of it, as it were, just as in real space, making digital space a tool for thinking and making that takes advantage of the whole of the virtuality continuum, but also of my body, my embodied knowledge of movement and making, and my ability to flexibly think about how to move to make in that space.

Embodied agency

Importantly, at its most extreme, digital space is potentially endless, sprawling in perpetuity forward in any direction where I am focusing my attention. An end exists because it is programmed as such. There is no real vertical being either that appeals to our consciousness of verticality and is ensured by a polarity of up and down – cellar and attic of a house, as it were. I can move up and down from my starting point, but there is no grounded presence necessarily leading me back to that starting point. I bring my understanding of embodiment into this extreme digital space when I work there, and the significance of this is that I also bring with me my intimate knowledge of real space and action into that digital space, too. This concerns my small movements and broad and sweeping actions, but it also shows how my understanding of space and action are deeply rooted in the real and my past experiences. Gaston Bachelard formulates it well when he states:

> [T]he house we were born in becomes imbued with dream values which remain after the house is gone. Centers of boredom, centers of solitude,

centers of daydream group together to constitute the oneiric house which is more lasting than the scattered memories of our birthplace.

(Bachelard, 1994 [1948], p. 17)

For Bachelard, the real house, with its polarity of spaces and creation of rooms and spaces, affords us different perspectives for a phenomenology of the imagination (cf. Bachelard, 1994 [1948], p. 17). From here we find that, as digital space does not and cannot constitute a concentrated being nor appeal to our consciousness of centrality as in the real (cf. Bachelard, 1994 [1948], p. 17), I must be the bridge between real and digital space through my actions and flexible thinking of making. Knowing now what digital space is and how I can experience it, I need to look closer at how I experience agency there to come to terms with why these differences are important.

At this point, things become more intertwined, where non-essential and important differences seem to overlap when in the act of making. There is, also, a wide range of ways of experiencing making in digital space. I can understand this aspect of digital space and making, thereby comparing what it means to make in real and digital space, by using sculpture as an example. Sculpture is enclosed space, that is, enclosed by both the object and the space around it that it commands (Langer, 1953, p. 88). The full space that is created as this structure of space is not a space of direct vision. It is volume. And because volume is given to haptic experience more than visual experience, the business of all sculpture 'is to translate its data into entirely visual terms, i.e. *to make tactual space visible*' (Langer, 1953, p. 90). Sculpting in three-dimensional digital space affords me a significantly different way to make tactual space visible than in the real. Firstly, my actions are mediated into that digital space by an implement or by means of some sort of controller or translated into it through the primary or secondary device that registers my actions. The force of my actions is of no real consequence. And secondly, while how that space shows up to me and the characteristics of the art that I make there are linked, they are not the same. What the maker works for is to formulate import, an organisation of perceptual space just like all other realms of the plastic arts (cf. Langer, 1953, pp. 72–75). However, the qualities of digital space where the positing of things becomes possible is that which the maker works with. Those qualities are interchangeable, but also, importantly, unstable and ambiguous, so much so that they can affect the sculpture as the organisation of perceptual space. This ambiguousness is inherent in the system and interface and follows in all digital space. Even though non-essential, I can nonetheless come to feel that the experience of making in real and in digital space are very different in this regard.

To understand why, we can look to Langer. Langer's discussion about sculpting in real space is interesting, because she reveals how the intimate relationship between touch and sight has been a topic of interest since well before the development of digital space as we know it. Concentrating on making in three-dimensional visual space, this close relationship not only defines sculpture according to Langer; it also allows me to make tactile space visible as maker, as it visualises haptic experience, allowing me to touch it, as it were, through vision. So close can visual-haptic experience be that when imagining an object, I can feel the weight of the object in my hand, its curvatures, and command of space even though I am touching nothing and only looking at my hands. In this way, things in digital space, too, can become a kinetic realm of tangible volumes (cf. Langer, 1953, p. 90), even though digital sculpture, like sculpture in the real, does not exist for touch or haptic experience; it exists for our vision alone (Langer, 1953, p. 92).

Bringing Merleau-Ponty into this discussion, we find resonance for the link between the different perceptions in his thoughts concerning synaesthesia, where we can read and feel a material's tactile and physical modalities through observing it visually (Merleau-Ponty, 1962 [2012], pp. 237–239). In this sense, sculptural making demands a form of advanced kinaesthetic knowledge which is made all the more evident in digital space. Let it be clear, though, that the link between visual and haptic experience is not some strange phenomenon for making, if we are to take Merleau-Ponty onboard, but part and parcel of human perception of the world:

> Synesthetic perception is the rule and, if we do not notice it, this is because scientific knowledge displaces experience and we have unlearned seeing, hearing, and sensing in general in order to deduce what we ought to see, hear, or sense from our bodily organization and from the world as it is conceived by the physicist.
>
> (Merleau-Ponty, 1962 [2012], p. 238)

We see things as hard, we hear things as rough, and we can even smell things as wet even though we have made it a habit to not theorise about these links. These natural connections are brought to the fore in Merleau-Ponty's extreme synaesethetic, who, in a case study, links sound and colour in disconcerting ways when not merely telling us 'that he has a sound and a color at the same time: it is the sound itself that he sees, at the place where colors form' (Merleau-Ponty, 1962 [2012], p. 238). While his example might be a radical form of synaesthesis, it nonetheless illustrates how closely intertwined different perceptions of the same thing can be. Similarly, it seems perfectly reasonable that I can feel the presence of a shape that I am moulding with empty space in my hands. Working with my object as it sits in digital space, my visual and tactile forming of space can present itself to me as totally intertwined. I know how to move myself and my tools, what its shape looks and feels like, even though I cannot otherwise attend to the shape through touch. With this synaesthetic relationship in play, I can continue articulating my form in digital space.

Even though it is the rule and natural, this does not mean that it must not or cannot be developed, strengthened through learning processes and by purposely becoming more aware of our surroundings. The professional sculptor knows how to form the object in visible, digital space, much like the professional violinist knows how to position their fingers to produce a succession of sounds and structure time through music in their intentional manner. Keogh refers to the jazz pianist David Sudnow when attempting to unpack how kinaesthetic knowledge is developed through the structure of videogames, and points for this reason to how Sudnow acquired the knowledge needed to become a competent jazz pianist (Sudnow, 1978 [2001], p. 15, in Keogh, 2018, p. 128):

> . . . [Sudnow] describes the transition he underwent from relying on his eyes to determine where his fingers needed to go on the piano keyboard to allowing those keys instead to become 'places towards which the appreciative fingers, hand, and arm are aimed' . . ... Sudnow gained a sense of the keys' locations in space by repetitively moving toward them, developing what he calls 'an embodied way of accomplishing distance' . . ... Jazz music, for Sudnow, is first and foremost 'particular ways of moving from place to place'.
>
> (Keogh, 2018, p. 127)

In this we find that Sudnow's movement through practice came to be closely associated with sound. Surely, so close is the specific movement-sound relationship as a professional, that the jazz pianist when playing doesn't stop to contemplate movement when intentionally structuring time through sound: Sound is movement and movement is sound.

But, where Sudnow's insights are relevant to art as well, Keogh only goes so far as to bring to the fore Sudnow's understanding of the key difference between learning movement in videogames and playing jazz piano; that is, the speed at which Sudnow was 'able to incorporate the actions demanded of the videogame, whereas learning the flourishes and improvisations of jazz piano took many years' (Keogh, 2018, p. 88). And as the creative arts are beyond the scope of his research, Keogh for reasonable reasons doesn't go far enough in unpacking the possibilities here. Nonetheless, the pianist example begins to illuminate the advanced kinaesthetic knowledge needed for sculpting. Like the pianist's understanding of movement and sound, in making art, so close are kinaesthetic, haptic, and visual aspects of bodily knowledge that surely they do not necessarily show up individually as such. That connection, too, is without doubt an awareness that has been strengthened by experience. Not only can we become more aware of these connections in general, but we can also intentionally develop them and strengthen how we aesthetically perceive the world through making, aesthetic awareness, purposeful practice, and intentional repetition. Just like those who have to train themselves to read and understand architectural plans to be able to see the building in the plans and the space in them at the same time, as if with double sight, some must strengthen their perception and awareness of making objects in digital space through working with making in the real.

This explains why when planning to bring a thing into the real that I might question my perception of my object in digital space, but I do not question the making of the form. To perceive a thing is to see the thing in situ, due to the articulative act of transitioning a work from the digital to the real: Remembering that Noë states that 'Paintings are material and their materiality counts' (Noë, 2015, loc. 3066), I agree in reference to the articulative act of transitioning a work from the real to the digital sphere, and I also agree in terms of the maker's uptake of the digital or physical work and the full body of its import after that transitioning. Therefore, I can still have an unsatisfactory sensory connection with the possibility of the digital space object when finished making in digital space, because when translating the thing into a different material, it changes its relation to me and others, its aesthetic being, and its import (cf. Langer, 1953, p. 81). But also, if I do not have sufficient embodied multimodal knowledge of digital space and its corresponding actual forms and materials in the real, I cannot see the object as one whole. Given the opportunity to explore the materials and things as they show up in real and then digital space, though, I would soon make in digital space, appreciating the characteristic range of semblance of space available to it, and seeing the things I make there, too, as if with double sight. As such, this links up to how mock-ups and clay models are devices to amplify the powers of my imagination and mind's eye, not replace them, so that I can get even closer to the object in the making process, when my intention is to bring it into the real and use it to solve more mundane practicalities of making things, to help discussions about the thing between the maker and the potential user of it.

Time and action

We have found so far that even though digital space is comprised of both physical equipment and software, we can experience digital space as different even though sometimes braided together with real space. I cannot, nor do I want to, completely immerse myself in digital space when making there, and I take a co-attentive stance, paradoxically staying fully attentive in both worlds at the same time. This does not undermine how I experience (and want to experience) myself as present in digital space, since it is my natural and learned perceptions of experiences that allow me to be in an artistic process in that digital space. So, while embodied space and embodied agency are non-essentially different in digital and real space, we are closer to identifying what which is the reason for the experienced differences. What is it, exactly, that differentiates real and digital space when making? Is it the glitches sometimes experienced in digital space that throw me out of my art process, that make the experience of making there different? Or is it the lags and lack of updates that are the culprit? The purpose of this final discussion is to uncover exactly what makes making in digital space different, even though not essentially so. We cannot fully address digital space as artistic space from a pedagogical perspective without having come closer to understanding these differences.

To do this, we will go back to the experience of making in digital space. Recalling our introductory analyses of the drawing experience, we see that the fly in the ointment is not the delays, jitters, bugs, and glitches one would firstly, and rightfully, suspect. To illustrate how this is so, consider this: I dwell in my digital pencil the same way as I dwell in my tools in the real. When drawing digitally, my pencil touches the drawing surface just a fraction of a hair above the drawing that is taking form because I am not drawing on the drawing surface, but rather on the glass surface covering it. When I hold a pencil and draw in the real, the pencil sits in my hand and, when I draw, the action is directly chronicled by a line. The pencil-drawn line could be comically long, and the line would still be chronicled instantaneously. When drawing in digital space, my pencil and my line as a chronicle and testimony of time never truly meet, like two magnets repelling each other. Drawing fast, especially with simple digital devices, that distance is made all the more visible to me. The line seems to pop up out of nowhere or chase my pencil, creating my drawing out of its own memory without me remembering exactly where my hand has been and what line had been made. I become unsure of what to concentrate on; my line, my pencil on the surface, or the movement I am just about to make. Drawing on a digital surface demands that I am more cognisant of the making moments and ripples of time that have just passed, to be able to push forward with my drawing. This is partly a processing lag, when the programme can't compute my actions fast enough and the machine increasingly falls behind, and as such something that is getting increasingly less visible due to technological developments, but it is also linked directly to the tool. No matter how advanced the programme itself becomes, unless the physical tool is changed so that the area of action is on or inside the surface, frustratingly, the drawing implement and the line can never meet.

In comparison, we see that there is an immediate and actual response in real material which we learn to expect from the very onset of life by making various marks on the world. Those are mediated or translated into digital responses in digital space. The close relationship between visual and haptic perception and kinaesthetic knowledge from the real when making can be disturbed by this mediation. Because of this, the indwelling in my tools over time while making, the rich space of time before and after the act of making, and the analytic and contemplative taking of time in making must be attended to afresh when thinking about making in digital space. However frustrating and going against the grain of most life experience it may be, dealing with a tool-based distance is nonetheless familiar to me. Thinking back to our example of working with silver, while there are certainly instances when one would engage directly with the materials through tools, such as sawing, filing, dapping, and doming, soldering clearly requires a different sort of connection with the materials. This process is not physical in the same way, nor do I experience it as instantaneous. I pick up on information such as the look of the surface and the colour of the flame and incorporate it into my tacit knowledge about the speed and height which I must pass the flame over my piece to work with the materials in this or that way. As such, this process is neither a direct chronicle of time, such as that of my pencil-drawn line, nor an immediate testament to the flow of thought, intention, and action. There is a type of lag to it; a lag which I learn to incorporate into using a torch. Just as I do with my digital drawing implement, being able to anticipate that familiar, tool-based lag is essential for me to be able to dwell in my tools (cf. Crick, 2011, p. 265). Frustrations that follow the drawing implement and the line never touching can merely be a reflection of my lack of familiarity or insufficient internalising of that lag and working that lag into my dialectical making process. Frustrating as it is, lagging can be incremental or jumpy, and outright annoying, but they are common.

Is it that a disruption to a familiar lag could disturb my flow of making and make it more difficult for me to remain aware and present in digital space? For the most part, though, there are lags in all digital space; it is just that we don't notice them until we make on a platform with fewer, shorter lags. As with my drawing example, I am dependent on having embodied knowledge about the interval between my bodily movement and the action I am able and intending to make in that digital space, even if that interval does increase incrementally. For this reason, unexpected lagging and body incongruity experienced when moving about in digital space is disconcerting. For example, when moving in digital space, if my head suddenly does not align with my hands or I briefly experience my hands as a little too far apart or too far from the object I am working on (cf. Weeks, 2021, p. 28). However slight that incongruity may be, those experiences constitute a disruption in time and the flow of action from my mental gaze, unsettling my dwelling in my tools and my subjective viewpoint, and making it harder for me to focus on my presence in digital space. Nonetheless, I am capable of shifting quickly back and picking up where I left off once the incongruity is resolved, much like drawing in the real when my pencil tip suddenly breaks, or the pearl of paint fails to release from my paintbrush. The sum of this leads us to suspect that it is not necessarily getting cast out of digital space and other immersion difficulties, nor lagging or user experience issues, that are our core concern in relation to making in digital space.

The core of our concern may in fact not preside in digital space alone at all. I suggest that the reason making in digital space is experienced as different is because of the ecology shared between the space and tool and the maker. Looking back on how materials play into art processes, we found that the maker and materials comprise an unambiguous ecology, which at the same time afforded a wide range of actions. Much like the pianist's hands and the violinist's fingers. The nature of digital space, as built from equipment and systems, adds ambiguity to that relationship precisely because digital space in and of itself is ambiguous in terms of what it can do and how it can read me as maker. If this is the case, as we will discuss in the next chapter, then it has significant pedagogical implications as well as implications for the role of the teacher in the post-digital era.

Bibliography

Art Gallery of New South Wales Contemporary Collection (AGNSW). (2011). *Charlotte Moorman performs with Paik's TV cello: Charlotte Moorman performing with TV cello at the art gallery of NSW in 1976*. Art Gallery NSW/YouTube. https://youtu.be/-9lnbIGHzUM

Bachelard, G. (1994 [1948]). *The poetics of space*. Beacon Press.

Crick, T. (2011). The game body: Toward a phenomenology of contemporary video gaming. *Games and Culture, 6*(3), 259–269.

Eisner, E. (2006). Does arts-based research have a future? *Studies in Art Education, 48*(1), 9.

Keogh, B. (2018). *A play of bodies: How we perceive videogames*. MIT Press.

Langer, S. (1953). *Feeling and form: A theory of art*. Scribner.

Merleau-Ponty, M. (1962 [2012]). *Phenomenology of perception* (D. Landes, Trans.). Routledge.

Noë, A. (2015). *Strange tools: Art and human nature* (Kindle ed.). Hill and Wang.

Paul, C. (Ed.). (2016). *A companion to digital art*. John Wiley & Sons.

Saethre-McGuirk, E.M. (2021). An i for an eye: The collective shaping of experience in the age of machine-mediated art. In M. La Caze & T. Nannicelli (Eds.), *Truth in visual media: Aesthetics, ethics and politics*. Edinburgh University Press.

Saethre-McGuirk, E. (2022). Hvem tegner? In A.C. Hedberg & R. Lundgreen (Eds.), *Digital og analog tegning i museet* (pp. 11–31). Museumsforlaget.

Schreyach, M. (2015). Re-created flatness: Hans Hoffman's concept of the picture plane as a medium of expression. *Journal of Aesthetic Education*, *49*(1), 44–67.

Sudnow, D. (1978 [2001]). *Ways of the hand: A rewritten account*. MIT Press.

Weeks, J. (2021). Body coherence in curved-space virtual reality games. *Computers & Graphics*, *97*, 28–41.

4   Teaching the creative arts in the post-digital era

Bananas and mandolins

To sum up so far, we have found digital space to be different, but not essentially different, in terms of making things. I am present in that space through my actions, I experience my actions through fundamentally natural processes, and I familiarise myself with my range of action there, as in other areas of making. Once I fully dwell in my tools in digital space, I can begin to fully explore that which digital space alone affords the maker.

It is reasonable that the range of semblance of space available in digital space is different to any other choice of materials, hardware, or software, affecting the organising of its space. 'One cannot always do the same things with diverse materials', Langer bluntly stated (Langer, 1953, p. 85), and that would seem to be the case here, too.

> The translucency of glass allows the making and use of special color elements that paint on a wooden ground could never create; therefore glass painting and wood painting set the artist different problems and suggest different ideas to be brought to expression. It is sometimes said that glass and wood have 'different feelings.' They permit, and even command, quite distinct forms, and of course equally distinct ranges of vital import.
>
> (Langer, 1953, p. 85)

Similarly, digital space has its distinct range of vital import, which is grounded in the split personality of digital space comprising seemingly all materials, colours, tools, and expressions. The many personalities of digital space are not the same as many different ranges of vital import, though. Rather, its range of vital import is precisely that it has many personalities. Those personalities are ultimately all linked, permitting and even commanding similar forms with similar ranges of vital import. At least for the

DOI: 10.4324/9780429326264-4

time being, they all, visually, are of the same cloth. At the same time, it would be too hasty a conclusion to leave it at that, because digital space does not share the unambiguous ecology of, say, a pencil and paper. Digital space is an ambiguous ecology. The computer seems to constantly be trying to clean up and tidy away the ambiguities inherent to it. Therefore, although aspects of embodied space and action in digital space as we have studied so far are similar or familiar to making in the real, we have to look closer at how these aspects come together in the act of making to define the intrinsic ambiguity of digital space.

When I articulate through my process in the real, I am, as it were, communicating with my materials. However, in digital space, this communication seems both missing, in that there are no real materials, and paradoxically seems all the more amplified, as if digital space at times has its own agency in relation to my making process, taking over the work. This is different from when Snekkestad, commenting on how he collaborates with his saxophone, stated: 'You could say that I give agency to the instrument – play around with the idea of it having its own intentions' (Høffding & Snekkestad, 2021, p. 168). Instead, digital space seems more eager and able to articulate me, as it were, or enable me to make, and changes are constantly being made to it for it to better accommodate me. Sometimes, digital tools even make me better at doing what I would otherwise do in real space and with real materials. A simple example is my penmanship seen on digital interfaces. Never before has my calligraphy been as precise and balanced as when writing in digital space.

To explain why this is so, you have to take into consideration that when you make something with real materials, and if you have made enough of anything, you will soon find that as you articulate your form, you are not merely chronicling your actions in the material to have the material echoing your actions, regardless of what is at hand. Ultimately, your actions will reveal some imperfection in the pencil or paper, dead knots in the wood, or flaws in the marble. In time you learn to find or see these imperfections before they show up in the piece, so that you can work around them or incorporate them into your form, but for the most part, they are simply there, statically present, sometimes showing up through your intentional and unintentional actions. In the real, it is the minute differences of the materials and the process, resulting from resistance inherent in the materials understood by me as affordances and constraints, that drive my making forward. The shared space between me and my materials becomes unambiguous through this resistance. And, the affordances there are not open to more than one interpretation in a similar way as in digital space, because materials in the real do not fundamentally change. In digital space, the fragility of this relationship is revealed. In digital space, my materials and tools seem more likely monotone than not, and quite nearly perfect. The drawing surface is the drawing surface, the space is the space, and my tools therein constantly remain as such. But this is not digital space. Looking back on Merleau-Ponty (1962 [2012], p. 243), these are merely the setting in which things are arranged. The means whereby the positioning of things becomes possible is more than just the sum of the setting. Digital space is the means by which positioning becomes possible, but in being that, digital space is met by a conundrum of its own. There are a whole host of interpretations of me and my actions which must be processed, processed quickly, and processed correctly. The baseline that all action must be processed, understood, and solved is the problem. Not that it cannot differentiate between the kinds of action present in my artistic making process. To illustrate this, we can imagine a simple event of drawing, followed by two alternative scenarios. The scenarios are both unrealistic and out of date, but precisely because of that, they bring to the fore the problem of making in digital space.

For our simple event, imagine drawing with a thin charcoal stick or vine charcoal. Holding the charcoal too far up and applying too much pressure will break it, leaving bigger and smaller chunks of charcoal and specks of charcoal dust in its wake. Being a notoriously messy medium, smudging and dusting on anything and everything, you would steer clear of that area in your drawing and try to leave it alone or carefully remove it before continuing.

As our first, albeit unrealistic, alternative scenario following this simple event, imagine that when you continue with the remains of your charcoal stick, the chunks and specks were to mirror your movements, continuing your drawing act from afar. As if detecting all of the charcoal touching the paper and operating on the assumption that the charcoal was for drawing, 'charcoal on paper' meant that my intention was for any charcoal on the paper to continue making marks. This is, to put it mildly, an unlikely scenario if you were to draw on paper in the real. In digital space, however, especially with older or less advanced drawing surfaces and programmes, it is more probable that my surface would pick up on other parts of my hand or, alternatively, radically misinterpret the placement of my line on the surface, mistakenly reading the new line as my continued, intended line. The result is similar; my hand continues to draw, and the new line, it seems, continues to copy my movements and draw, too.

Drawing programmes have long since solved this practical problem, and for the most part, drawing programmes and surfaces are well able to differentiate between my implement and my other hand, and they have cleaned the programmes of glitches to try to place my line directly under my pen. However, keeping this scenario in mind brings us to our second scenario. In our second scenario following the simple charcoal breaking on real paper event, I am drawing with the broken charcoal stick in my right hand, only to want to intentionally smudge the charcoal specks with my left thumb without lifting my right hand and disturbing the line. Perhaps I even want to use both hands, because the unexpected breaking event opened up new avenues to artistically explore by drawing with both hands, ambidextrously (cf. Høffding & Snekkestad, 2021, pp. 171–172). In digital space, however, the event and the second scenario actions that follow are in all likelihood outside of what we have come to anticipate as the general, expected usage of my digital surface, meaning that I cannot necessarily use both hands independently of one another. However, this can be solved, too, by communicating through my controller that that is what I specifically wanted to do, if I have the appropriate equipment or by working through a programme that is set up for working with more than just one hand, which of course is possible.

This simple event and two following scenarios, unlikely as they are, illustrate an epistemological and aesthetic problem of working in digital space which extends beyond the characteristics and range of semblance of space available to us in it. It relates to the constant tidying away of resistance and the changing character of digital space, which is altogether a different problem than my charcoal sticks breaking or even working with a torch. It relates to the nature of how that space comes into being. Where there is a more ambiguous ecology for making in digital space, there is ironically less room for my intentional and unintentional creative exploration and dwelling in digital space.

Our event and unlikely scenarios remind us of the understanding and then solving of the framing problem, much like the one early AI researcher Marvin Minsky was faced with when dealing with the conundrum of why computers couldn't comprehend simple stories understood by 4-year-olds. Understanding that it wasn't simply a problem of not having all of the information, his commentor Hubert L. Dreyfus identified the real problem as *not* that of not storing and organising sufficiently millions of facts, but rather of not being able to know which facts were relevant (Dreyfus, 2005, p. 48). Murray Shanahan illustrates the problem well in his presentation of the frame problem (2016):

> A process might indeed be able to index everything the system knows about, say, bananas and mandolins, but the purported mystery is how it could ever work out that, of all things, bananas and mandolins were relevant to its reasoning task in the first place.

Having since solved the many programming and design problems such as the framing problem and that which would have led to both scenarios in terms of making, like my unintentional extra drawing actions and unannounced double hand gestures, my digital tools and programmes have been rid of art's own bananas and mandolins and, quite possibly, bicycles and bull's heads, as well.

Through painstakingly being tested for design flaws, usability tested for common wrongful gestures, and checked in relation to multi-gesture usage, both the physical design of my tools (e.g. Norman 1988 [2013]) and the perceived design of my programme (e.g. Kreimer, 2005) are meticulously checked and eventually fixed for the better. As such, digital space today can correct my unintentional actions without me having to tell it what to ignore, and it can ignore my seemingly unintentional actions given that I have the opportunity to tell it to do so. But in that, it has also increasingly taken away a creative resistance that inherently resides in materials in the real and the unambiguous ecology there. Its uniformity is both a relief and a regret, in that the imperfections I come across in the real can be an important source of resistance that I use as a part of my creative process. Not only that, but the aim of digital space development would seem to be to irradicate this resistance altogether and enable digital space to constantly interpret my actions as flawless, with only perfect gestures, and as exactly as one would expect them to be. It would seem, then, that that is the fate of digital space. In this sense, making in digital space is different.

While it is unfortunate, it is at the same time an impossible predicament to be in: driven forth by the expectation that the experience of digital space will be of 'high quality on all situations and contexts' (Boavida et al., 2013, p. 1606), and recognising that our understanding of what is high quality changes dramatically over time. Indeed, there seems to be a push to improve immersion in relation to serious gaming and other professional uses of virtual technology in particular, because, for certain professions and areas of use such as virtual training, remote presence, and tele-surgery at least, seamless and smooth immersion is clearly important (Awed et al., 2013, p. 1621). Ultimately, though, in that my making art and appreciation of art is not derailed by the possibilities of imperfection that lay within and throughout every artistic endeavour, I have no need for, nor do I want my process and work to be perfect. It is in the imperfections, as they were, in the performance or the variations in the work's theme that the full extent of the possible import is made available to me. Slight variations can be grounds for significant differences in the end piece as meaningful. The only truly viable path of development of digital space is not to make it more perfect, but to accept my messy, imperfect, human way of being.

The lack or reduction of resistance is in this light an important pedagogical loss, as well as one that has implications because it alters our understanding of digital space's affordances and constraints. Elliot Eisner expressed the importance of resistance well when contemplating the future of arts-based research in terms of writing:

> The heart of the problem resides for the students in the relationship between seeing and expressing. Seeing is necessary in order to have a content to express. Expression is necessary to make public the contents

of consciousness, and so what we have here is an imaginative transformation of a perceptual event that is imbued with meaning whose
features and significance the students try to transform into language
capable of carrying that meaning forward. . . . Somehow the writer
must find a way within the affordances and constraints of a linguistic
medium to try to create the structural equivalent of the experience.

(Eisner, 2006, p. 13)

The key in real space is using the affordances and constraints as agential poles, something to hold on to and use to project the work forward,
points that sharpen thinking about what is to be expressed while in the
making moment. Lack of resistance in and of itself is not an agential pole.
By eradicating resistance in an ambiguous ecology, we are increasingly
making digital space an odd creative companion, especially in a pedagogical setting. The problem, then, with the framing problem from the point
of view of making is that it wasn't a problem to begin with. It was an
opportunity. And for this reason, the framing problem from the aesthetic
perspective wasn't necessarily something to be solved. It was something
to be explored.

At the same time, this pedagogical loss is not rectified by giving pupils
and schools old equipment nor by necessarily equipping them with high-end
haptic suits, either. Acknowledging that digital space is constantly being
refined in this way, then, the task has to be to understand how best to situate constructive learning situations in that space. While professionals, well
skilled in working in that space, might be beyond this problem, we cannot
assume that learners do not thrive under the presence of resistance as one of
several agential poles, but one of few readily available to the pupil. There
are also conceivably other downsides to lack of resistance. Eisner identified
learning to think within the constraints and affordances of materials as one
of the conditions that 'contribute significantly to the development of cognition' (Eisner, 2006, p. 236). Met by new tasks through different constraints
and affordances, pupils have to flexibly and intelligently think of new ways
to address their aesthetic task (cf. Eisner, 2006, p. 237). By increasingly
removing this resistance, one could also argue that we are losing the pedagogical possibility of learning to contend with any tool or situation within
the constraints and affordances around us (cf. Eisner, 2006, p. 237).

In that resistance can be a tool by which the pupil develops their making
process, removing resistance without compensating for it might even be
counterproductive. It then becomes the task of the teacher to compensate
for that lack of resistance in pedagogical making processes. In this sense,
making in digital space is closer to an improvised performance, an articulative act which is in constant dialogue with the tool, the materials, and the

space. This is significant because it entails that the teacher must address or even strengthen and pull to the fore other possibilities to interact with in the making process, by which the pupil can go deeper into their project or stay, as it were, negotiating that which is available to them, wherever they are in their process.

The pupil addresses this space by seeing and being in the world and expressing meaningful import through the materials at hand. Like any medium, digital space has its own range of possibilities and vital import – its own feeling, as Langer commented on the particularities of all arts (Langer, 1953, p. 85). The pupil brings their ever-important physical experiences of real world engagements into the more and less digital space. Once familiar with and comfortable in that digital space, the pupil can explore the possibilities for making there. Those possibilities are like no other and allow for an articulation unique to that space; looping back, as it were, with new and different ways of looking at the world, enabling us unlike any other material to think differently about our being in the world, and empowering us to think sideways about old problems, too. As such a higher-order meta-conceptual reflection, art and the process of making art engages the viewer and the maker on many levels, extending beyond the mere ability to use a tool or take or make a picture, however complex and difficult that may be. By continuously, or incrementally even, processing their actions to the better, digital space is also removing resistances. While this may be of no consequence for the professional, it does matter to the pupil.

Our aim now is to bring the banana and mandolin opportunity into terms of teaching. We are particularly interested in teaching the creative arts, and at that, specifically visual art, through the lens of the post-digital era. As such, while a matrix of actions mixing the pupil and the teacher as well as formal education and non-formal education figure in this discussion, our aim is undeniably linked to formal education pedagogy and the act of teaching art. In light of this, though, there are two things which are of paramount importance. The first is that, on a metalevel, school as an institution not only reflects, but is intrinsically part of the values from which it was formed. The second is that, on a microlevel, the creative arts are included in education in different ways and with different underlying intentions, which ultimately impact the alternative approaches to placing the creative arts in early childhood education and schools as well as in higher education programmes, such as in pre-service teacher education.

Explaining these points, firstly, we must recognise that all teaching is planned and takes place within a conceptual, social, cultural, political, and historical framework. How knowledge is identified, framed, and communicated, the aims of that learning journey, and the perceived intrinsic value of it, is all understood through that framework. Naturally, the situation is no different for teaching the creative arts or for art education in general, where even examples of significant differences at the coalface have been discussed (e.g. Atkinson, 2002, p. 137). In the introduction to her global research compendium on the impact of the arts in education, Anne Bamford (2006) illustrated this well when she struggled to define art education within the quantitative part of her research (Bamford, 2006, p. 10), inadvertently also struggling to define what creative arts teaching is or could be. She landed on a two-pronged definition of art education: Emphasising the aim of art education as to pass on cultural heritage to young people, and enable them 'to create their own artistic language and to contribute to their global development (emotional and cognitive)' (Bamford, 2006, p. 10). But in this, Bamford also underlined the need to interpret her quantitative findings through reference to qualitative case studies, clearly stating that 'What is seen as art in one culture is not defined as such in another' (Bamford, 2006, p. 10). This has direct implications for teaching, as in teaching content, the practice of teaching, and the aims of teaching, as well as genuinely having impact on the pupil, too.

Secondly, there is a difference between education in the arts and education through the arts. Bamford also encountered this difference in relation to her work on the global compendium, defining education in the arts as 'teaching in fine arts, music, drama, crafts, etc.' and education through the arts as 'the use of arts as a pedagogical tool in other subjects, such as numeracy, literacy and technology' (Bamford, 2006, p. 11). While I wholeheartedly embrace using the arts as a pedagogical tool for learning in other subjects, doing so cannot take the place of learning in the arts, and especially in visual art, which is fundamentally linked to developing the pupil's awareness of and ability to partake in an arts practice, that is an organisational and reorganisational practice for gaining a meta-perspective on our being in the world. This is not to say that both education in and through the arts does not have a positive impact on other aspects of pupils' educational achievements; which was also confirmed by Bamford (Bamford, 2006, p. 143). One could argue, even, that the downstream gains from learning to be in, work in, and negotiate digital space from an education in art point of view, are conceivably more significant in light of digitalisation strategies on national and international levels than has been understood up until now. Nonetheless, accepting that there is a difference between learning in and through the arts on a metalevel is not to be confused with how arts education, and hence creative arts teaching, is culture and context specific. Indeed, teaching through the arts can be culture and context specific, too. For this reason, I recognise that others can have overlapping interests in this discussion on teaching the creative arts in the post-digital era, even though my interest is firmly placed in teaching the creative arts as education in the arts.

Teaching as an improvisational microenvironment

We continue this discussion from the perspective of the pupil engaged in making art in digital space. In this we see that the pupil is now our maker, continuously developing their abstract and flexible thinking and understanding of aesthetic experiences, as well as developing their skills in this regard. In this, the pupil is engaged in an embodied process of space and action in a post-digital sense; a 'shift to new movements of emergent bodies, engaging in affectively charged relationships' (Leander, 2015, p. 436). This is important because it acknowledges how digital space can alter how pupils relate to making and what they make, not radically and instantly as soon as they enter that space, but slowly and incrementally as they constructively explore making in that space, being a significant shift nonetheless (cf. Ehret & Hollett, 2013, p. 111).

I also acknowledge the role of the teacher in teaching in this space. The role of the art teacher is not to deliver teaching, but rather to construe environments comprised of situations that the teacher and the pupils co-construct in an improvised activity, together (cf. Eisner, 2006, p. 47). However, not only is making in digital space an improvised performance of sorts, the act of teaching itself is fundamentally an improvisatory practice. As such, teaching in general has undeniable improvisational undertones that are a constant 'improvisatory dimension in successful classroom practice, as in all action' (McGuirk, 2021, p. 183). Action, classroom practice, and teaching art in digital space are intrinsically improvisational, distinguishing between the understanding that all action includes improvisation, that is, understanding action as a dichotomy of improvisation-planning, and the understanding that all action is intrinsically improvisatory, where 'the precise nature and scope of the improvisatory will be different in different cases' (McGuirk, 2021, p. 192). The precise nature and scope of the improvisatory is indeed different in the cases of all action, classroom practice, and teaching art in digital space. There are as such several layers of improvisatory practices taking place in the creative arts classroom, making the act of teaching there increasingly complex. In this light, Elliot Eisner's comment on teaching is all the more to the point: 'The surest road to hell in a classroom is to stick to the lesson plan, no matter what' (Eisner, 2002, p. 48).

This understanding of the fundamentally improvisatory nature of teaching, and subsequently of teaching art, links up with the needs that follow the post-digital era's imprecise virtual and non-virtual frontiers and ubiquitous communication. Indeed, understanding this connection leads to questioning practice and opening up for new approaches to teaching today. Kevin Leander addresses the emerging need for new ways of teaching when he seems to propose using improvisation not as much as a technique, but as an analogy for understanding what this new approach to teaching can mean in practice. Leander illustrated this approach as a way of being in time with children, comparing it to improvisational theatre: 'It was a tectonic shift toward learning-in-time, a shift that forced presence' (Leander, 2015, p. 437). In relation to teaching, he continues:

> Whereas the soul of representational, rationalistic frameworks is typically either/or, the soul of improvisation is and/and. . . . Perhaps the most common mindset and bodyset for improvisation is to act as if radically different realities that seem incommensurate are, in all possibility, filled with potential in their juxtaposition. Planning and unplanning . . . and/and Education as a site for possibility, in a world of moving spaces.
>
> (Leander, 2015, p. 437)

Angie Zapata et al. (2019) went further than using improvisation as an analogy and defined it as a concrete approach to teaching; 'an engaged relation with, or being with, the shifting texts, meanings, and affects entering the classroom, a relation that results in authentic instructional turns' (Zapata et al., 2019, p. 179). But where Zapata et al. concentrate on justice-oriented literacies closely linked to the world beyond the classroom walls, the creative arts teacher and the pupil working in digital space are simultaneously also concerned with a different source of reflection; that is, making in digital space. It isn't an event which the teacher can task themselves with bringing into the classroom for discussion and exploration in the same way as contemporary societal events can be brought into social and justice studies. It becomes the task of the teacher to design an environment for the pupils to constructively navigate digital space as it differs from making in the real, negotiating the space and bringing to light something meaningful.

Zapata's being with does not mean bringing something into the classroom only because it is new or different. Reflecting on the different ways or reasons that new media has been brought into art education, Zapata's being with implies that we do not bring digital space into the classroom only because it is a new technology enabling one to create and manipulate in making. Rather, it implies engaging with that which is new or different because of the impact it has on the world as the pupils know it. Because the pupils' concepts of reality are based on the works, spaces, communications, and connections, that is, the world generated by and in digital space (cf. Efland, 1990, p. 257), being with pupils in terms of visual art presumes that the teacher is also present in this world as part and parcel of their improvisatory practice.

Such an engaged relationship presumes different levels of co-making. The teacher being with the pupils in emerging relations in digital space entails an engaged relationship with the pupils in their act of making. The teacher must be able to work in that space and be together with the pupil in making, both practically and in terms of understanding this world. One such example of that is seen in this Swedish case study comment, from a classroom where the 'dichotomy between digital media- and manually-based art [had] been abolished' (Marner, 2013, p. 369):

> Pupils teach other pupils, including the teacher, and the sender and recipient relationship is constantly changing in character and position in the teaching. The teacher thinks, 'There are no teachers and pupils here. We are a group, with minimal hierarchies, that makes things'.
>
> (Marner, 2013, p. 365)

As an approach to teaching and pedagogical planning, being with the pupils suggests 'an openness to emerging pedagogies and learning and to the potential of putting different perspectives and realities into the [pedagogical] conversation' (Zapata et al., 2019, p. 180). In relation to making in digital space, this implies including other pupils in the co-making processes, making room for and including other perspectives in shared art processes, and simultaneously accepting the imprecise virtual maker/non-virtual maker frontier by including both those inside and outside the digital space in a common process. Not just a making situation for the pupil alone or between the pupil and the teacher, then, such co-creation invites pupils to be open to new insights and perspectives on making and the articulation of significant import together. In practice, for the teacher engaged in being with the pupils as they explore making in digital space, this entails seeing the pupil, the pupils, the plans, the space, and the world at once, and, in that, being able to pursue emerging lines of flight towards artmaking possibilities (cf. Zapata et al., 2019, p. 180).

Following this, the teacher must have knowledge of those emerging lines of flight as they can reveal themselves in digital space, which in turn implies seeing making in digital space as an improvised act within a pedagogical framework. This places significant demands on teachers' pedagogical content knowledge in order to enable the pupils' constructive exploration of digital space. That pedagogical content knowledge must naturally include the full breadth and width of contemporary artistic space, including lesser and greater degrees of digital space. This is confirmed in that all teaching can be understood as improvisatory, where it takes 'the form of a conversational navigation of the various responses which the various elements make possible' (McGuirk, 2021, p. 193). Thus, being able to teach in specific fields necessitates specialised content knowledge. In other words, the possibility of that conversational navigation demands that responses can be understood as relevant for the pedagogical situation at hand in the first place. As such, not only are the pupils themselves significant elements in that situation, but the objects, things, drawings, and undoubtably, digital space are, too.

In this, the teacher must both recognise the pupils' making in digital space as an improvisational act, and also themselves embrace the fundamental improvisatory nature of teaching in digital space as part of their range of competencies as an art teacher. This becomes the basis of the teacher's improvisational microenvironment, where the teacher plans for action, subsequently finds resistance to those plans, and improvises to 're-engage the situation as a space for possible action' (McGuirk, 2021, p. 194), which is in itself is made all the more complex by it being in response to the pupils' own improvisational microenvironments, taking it into service and understanding then what that can entail in terms of learning-in-time.

Once fully accepting the improvisatory nature of teaching, being with the pupils in terms of what that presumes as the basis for the teacher's practice, inviting co-making practices in the classroom, and understanding the competencies that are needed in the teacher for this to play out, the key is to identify the pupil's making process as it unfolds and potentially can unfold; that is, the nature and the scope of the pupil's improvisation in making in digital space. For this reason, while the pupil's making and the act of teaching visual art can be further studied through the lens of improvisation in general, we will look closer at these relationships specifically in terms of the improvisational microenvironment that is making and performing in the arts. Here, we take as our point of departure Snekkestad and Høffding's theoretical mapping of Snekkestad's performative system as it relates to free improvisation, to both understand the pupil's making situation and uncover the teacher's possibilities to navigate that space with the pupil.

A word must be offered on free improvisation at this early point, so that it is not confused with jazz improvisation in general or even traditional Western music, and to uncover significant points of similarity between free improvised performance and making and teaching the creative arts in digital space. Having multiple intercultural points of origin, there are 'no explicit rules of engagement . . .: no rhythm, no melody, no scale, no chords, none of the usual building blocks [of music]' (Høffding & Snekkestad, 2021, p. 164) that define the structure and process of free improvisation. More so than delivering a piece of composed music, free improvisation is about musical communication (Høffding & Snekkestad, 2021, p. 164). It is within this aesthetic landscape that we can see that there are distinct differences between free improvisation and making and teaching art, although we can also see some significant similarities. In terms of making art, both free improvisation and making art can, and often do, relate in some manner to other artistic references and instrument techniques, but while playing or making one can also go beyond these, emphasising the communicative import of the piece rather than references and techniques. In terms of teaching visual art specifically, free improvisation and teaching the creative arts will often have less interest in delivering (a musical product) than in creating (something which is aesthetically meaningful to the maker but also to the audience). This mental shift from what is made to the act of making is important in teaching the creative arts in that it attends to developing aesthetic awareness and embodied knowledge related to making art. In addition, free improvisation and teaching the creative arts emphasise the uniquely explorative nature of the arts fluidly working within a framework of improvisational action. While in teaching the creative arts one rarely achieves with one's pupils reaching the same depths in the improvisational act as professional free improvisation musicians do, the teacher will often strive to open up the art process in this way to their pupils.

Høffding and Snekkestad visualise Snekkestad's performative system while in the improvisational act as a complex weave comprised of three different stances inside a circle: a map of sorts, where each stance in turn is divided up into a number of different perspectives (Høffding & Snekkestad, 2021, p. 167). The perspectives are agential poles that Snekkestad can grab on to, so to speak, in order to alter the course of the improvisational performance as it unfolds (Høffding & Snekkestad, 2021, p. 166). These become different techniques Snekkestad uses to move forward with his performance, which can be compared to the techniques that the pupil becomes aware of through the learning situation designed by the teacher, where the aim is to develop aesthetic awareness and embodied knowledge related to making art. As such, both the pupil and the professional are engaged in an improvisational microenvironment, where Høffding and Snekkestad recognise this microenvironment from the perspective of the professional as being wholly contained in one moment:

> [t]he entire circle represents the performative system, that is, Snekkestad as fused with his performance at any given moment. Beyond the circle is what spatially lies outside of the performance (the toilets at the venue or his flat), and temporally before or after the performance.
> (Høffding & Snekkestad, 2021, p. 166)

While a detailed presentation and analysis of the 13 agential poles in Snekkestad's performative system is beyond the scope of the argument at hand, a short presentation of these poles is nonetheless necessary. The outer ridge of the circle seems to be held in place by the first stance - that is,

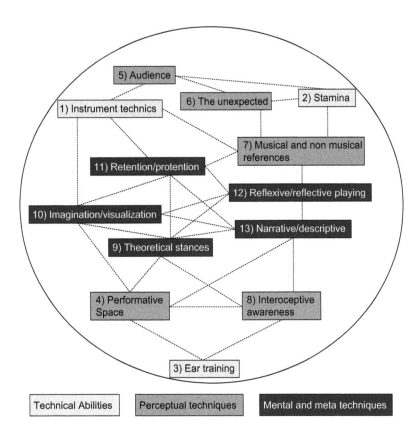

Figure 4.1 Snekkestad's performative system
Source: Høffding & Snekkestad (2021)

by technical abilities. This first stance is divided into three corresponding agential poles: instrument techniques, stamina, and ear training. These are core discipline-related abilities addressing the instrument, the musician, and the musician's knowledge of music. Following the first stance, the second stance is perceptual techniques. This stance is divided into five corresponding agential poles: performative space, audience, the unexpected, musical and non-musical references, and interoceptive awareness. These agential poles have in common being related to the world around the musician in the act of playing, as well as the musician using their own body as a tool to not only play, but also manipulate the playing possibilities of the instrument.

They are close to the outer ring of the system, but also reach further into the performative system, indicating how the poles to a certain degree build on each other, going deeper into the performative act. Lastly, the third stance is mental and meta techniques. Also divided into five agential poles, these are theoretical stances, imagination/visualisation, retention/protention, reflexive/reflective playing, and narrative/descriptive. Høffding and Snekkestad placed these agential poles closest to the centre of the interactive performative system because they are the least dependant on or react to the other poles. It is here that the musician 'tweaks his mind to squeeze out new musical material', but it is also where the musician forms and breaks musical habits in a 'totalised kind of insight that what you are playing now always is in response to everything you have ever played before' (Høffding & Snekkestad, 2021, p. 174).

As useful as it is in a professional context, however, I suggest a different visualisation to help organise our ideas on the exploration of digital space in light of teaching the creative arts in the post-digital era. As opposed to a ring with increasingly central agential poles which literally centre the professional creative act, I suggest visualising diving into a body of water. Here the pupil, together with the teacher, strives to reach deeper in their creative process, and consequently uses those agential poles to go further into their process.

The pedagogical exploration of digital space as artistic space

My alternative visualisation is clearly inspired by Snekkestad's own account of his childhood memories of diving underwater at the Norwegian archipelago (Høffding & Snekkestad, 2021, p. 175). However, Snekkestad's account was merely a means to explain visualising scenarios in and through music and thus connecting imagination to artistic visualisation as an agential pole in its own right. And, his account only concerned this one agential pole (imagination/visualisation) and not the map as a whole, whereas I fully appropriate Høffding and Snekkestad's stances and perspectives – that is, the whole map – in my diving analogy. In addition, intentionally or not, Høffding and Snekkestad's systems map visually reveals that all of the agential poles are readily available to the professional performer at once, just like reading a map of mountainous terrain instead of standing in that terrain. At the same time, while improvisation is, simply put, hard work, making and correspondingly learning and teaching visual art is hard work, too; if not harder. Neither the pupil nor the teacher on behalf of the pupil can see all of the valleys and mountain peaks at once, no matter how familiar the teacher is with the landscape. When temporally and physically in that making moment (cf. Høffding & Snekkestad, 2021, p. 166), the pupil may not be able to reach down into the deeper strata of making or see the whole mountainous terrain at once because the map is simply not fully available to them yet. The teacher with their pedagogical content knowledge knows what such a landscape is like and can help situate the pupil in their effort, but it is ultimately the pupil's endeavour that will get them there (cf. Eisner, 2002, p. 47).

Seemingly dismayed by the circle presentation, Høffding and Snekkestad suggested that a three-dimensional image, where all of the stances and agential poles where equally connected to one another, would have been a better graphic representation (Høffding & Snekkestad, 2021, p. 166). But this is not the same as shifting the circle visualisation out for the diving analogy. In my diving analogy, the stances exist as different strata of water, only to be penetrated by agential poles poking down to different depths and agential poles sticking up from the seabed at different heights. Appropriating Høffding and Snekkestad's three main different stances, then, and viewing these as strata of water, we can identify them as technical abilities, perceptual techniques, and mental and meta techniques. Thinking through this analogy of diving in the water, the pupil can use the agential poles to explore the material and act of making at that stratum or, by propelling themselves as it were, going deeper the between the strata and in between the poles as well. Visualising agential poles literally as poles is helpful in that it makes it easy to see the pupil approaching these poles and using them to add or decrease their making momentum and change the structure of their making activity, just like one could grab on to a pole to slingshot or propel oneself in a new direction or slow oneself down when moving.

In that this diving analogy is closely tied to the performative system, understanding the complexity of the performative system is necessary to use it to fully come to terms with making in digital space and teaching the creative arts in the post-digital era. Even though a first glance at the diving analogy illustration reminds us that some strata are more difficultly attained than others when making art as a creative pedagogical effort, which is both a useful and important insight, we cannot go further without giving the system some more consideration. Specifically, we are interested in the agential poles in terms of the relationship between them, the diving analogy as it attends to the microenvironments of improvisation in making in digital space, and lastly, the specific agential poles – that is, the links between each stance, linking the strata together – which are relevant in relation to the ambiguity of digital space.

A visual analysis of the performative system as a general system in this regard reveals that the three main stances/strata and their corresponding perspectives/agential poles both increase and become increasingly

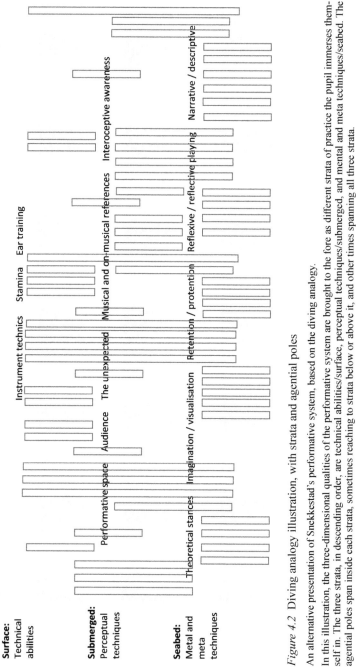

Figure 4.2 Diving analogy illustration, with strata and agential poles

An alternative presentation of Snekkestad's performative system, based on the diving analogy.

In this illustration, the three-dimensional qualities of the performative system are brought to the fore as different strata of practice the pupil immerses themself in. The three strata, in descending order, are technical abilities/surface, perceptual techniques/submerged, and mental and meta techniques/seabed. The agential poles span inside each strata, sometimes reaching to strata below or above it, and other times spanning all three strata.

intertwined as one moves from the stances/strata of technical abilities to perceptual techniques and further to mental and meta techniques. In other words, the amount of possible agential poles made available to the maker not only increase in number as one moves deeper into the improvisational act, but these poles also become more woven together, making it possible to play off of them and stay, as it were, longer and deeper in the making act in digital space. Next, we find that a visual analysis also clearly shows a significant and complex relationship between 'the analytical ability to understand the schematics of the current music and its musical potentials' (Høffding & Snekkestad, 2021, p. 174) (theoretical stance) and responding to that current musical situation through protention/leaning back from and retention/leaning into musical possibilities while playing (retention/protention). All other agential poles, nearly, extend out from that relationship, or alternatively, lead to that relationship; a relationship which is also deeply situated within the improvisational act. In terms of making in digital space, this is the ability to understand the image or object as it is becoming and its aesthetic potentials and responding to those possibilities while in the act of making. Furthermore, it is especially interesting to note that while stamina and physical form in relation to using one's instrument (technical abilities), the audience as an agential pole that can be used to shape the music (perceptual techniques), and unexpected events (perceptual techniques) are least capable of moving the improvisational act into the deeper levels of improvisation, they are an important part of the system structure. It is precisely the relationship between the musician/music and the audience that completes a piece. So much so that the critique, as it is used in art education, is an essential exercise to learn to understand how other people see and understand one's work. It is also significant for making in digital space, in that unexpected events and ambiguities are condensed or even removed, thus shifting the balance of making in relation to other agential poles; making being able to actively stay in digital space and co-creation all the more important. Lastly, and of special interest in relation to teaching visual art, the path with the most agential poles as one moves from the more planned to the more improvisational act, takes one from using instrumental technics (technical abilities) and musical and non-musical references (perceptual techniques) to regulating the playing. In effect, thus revealing the unique complexity underlying the seemingly simple act of making something meaningful and of import.

As one moves deeper into the performative act, more opportunities for improvisation reveal themselves, eventually leading to where the performer can both read and react to the music as it is being made, keeping deep in the improvisational act. In light of teaching the creative arts in digital space, though, this visual analysis also shows how perceptual techniques are affected in digital space; they are still beneficial poles for aesthetic inquiry, but differently so. The importance of the other agential poles, or the presence of these as they show up as and in other elements, compensating for the lack of bodily resistance, the different ways in which digital space shows up to the pupil, and the constant structuring of ambiguities and dampening of unexpected events when making in digital space, becomes clear. In lieu of the unexpected as it otherwise shows up in materials in the real, the pupil in their improvisational microenvironment must rely on being able to stay in digital space as artistic space, to work openly and together with their peers and teacher in the act of making and in reflection exercises, and to bring in other references as agential poles. And, in light of teaching the creative arts in the post-digital era, then, based on the performative system and this visual analysis, we find that an emphasis on co-creation and reflection, using, recognising, and reacting to aesthetic and non-aesthetic associations and references in making, and developing familiarity with all forms of artistic space, is the most pedagogically rewarding avenue to design the pupil and teacher's pedagogical making situations around.

Digital space cannot be fully understood without real world experiences to build from. The pupil's engagement with digital space is in this sense a familiar improvisational microenvironment, where the pupil engages in making art at different levels. The agential poles are opportunities to explore the flow of making as a means to go deeper into the creative act. In teaching we aim to construe situations with and around the pupil and pupils, where they can explore the flow of making, recognising that the strata and agential poles are all linked together as one body of water. The diving analogy, then, clearly shares Høffding and Snekkestad's organisational structure of the three strata (cf. Høffding & Snekkestad, 2021, p. 166), but does so while recognising that they are of one and the same structure.

At the surface, technical abilities as the first strata are essential; forming, planned, but also necessary to be able to make anything at all, let alone to dive down into the deeper strata of making. In terms of making in digital space, these technical abilities at first relate to familiarising the pupils with the appropriate tools so that they can take them into service for making simple forms, objects, and things. The pupils bring with them their rich and diverse experience of working with real materials. It also relates to the pupils' stamina and ability to stay in the creative act and work with their art and design processes in digital space; that is, keeping their awareness of the real world at an appropriate distance in conjunction with digital space. Lastly, it relates to the importance of developing knowledge about aesthetic form and being able to recognise form against a greater aesthetic, historical, and cultural backdrop. Technical abilities as the surface strata alone nonetheless offer the teacher less opportunity to make situations for the pupil to propel themselves between its agential poles, being as they are few and spread apart. Technical abilities as the surface are the very starting point of the pupil's engagement. Getting deeper into the act of making by relating to the world around them when making, as well as using their own bodily experience as a tool to make and manipulate the making possibilities of digital space, is responding to digital space in its own right. Once past the initial demands of technical abilities, the pupil can increasingly address the perceptual techniques of making.

In comparison, mental and meta techniques as the seabed strata offer the pupil more agential poles to attend to, so that the pupil can more readily explore digital space and alter the course of their making process therein. However, while the seabed agential pole points are the most intertwined, it is hard work for the pupil to attain and use as these points for developing their making process. Perhaps for this reason, they can also afford the most rewarding sense of flow in the act of making. Diving further down towards the totally immersed strata, we can borrow from Snekkestad's account of his childhood memory of diving in the archipelago to further illuminate this idea:

> I had this image of me taking a breath, diving under water and found this meditative state of mind, then, down in ocean, I'd gradually open my eyes and look for instance at the seabed . . . the sunlight penetrating the ocean . . . things floating by. . . [I]it became a very visual way of entering a state of trance.
>
> (Høffding & Snekkestad, 2021, p. 175)

It seems fitting that Snekkestad himself referred to this imaginative visualisation as a state of trance, in that the performative system clearly reveals how the performer can play off the intricate weave between the agential poles in the improvisation act at this level and, as it were, actively stay in the flow of making.

The pupil's making in digital space becomes navigable as an intense and strenuous perpetual shifting between awareness-of and getting on with their skills, calling on different experiences and awarenesses of real space. Co-creation in making and collaborative reflection and assessment activities puts making on display for the pupil. We find resonance for this in Snekkestad's account of being with the audience:

> [The music] is literally out there in the room with the audience, and Snekkestad reports listening to it as if sitting among them. This experience surely is at the heart of . . . the kinds of out-of-body experiences

[that some musicians report . . .] because the sense of being among the audience at the same time is an experience of not being the central locus of the music.

(Høffding & Snekkestad, 2021, p. 171)

In this way, the pupils and the teacher are being with each other while making in digital space, so much so that it is not an unspecifiable art of making (cf. Polanyi, 1969, p. 53) which cannot be specified in detail, transmitted by prescription or passed on apart from by example. It becomes something which is shared and developed in the pedagogical improvisational microenvironment.

Bibliography

Atkinson, D. (2002). *Art in education: Identity and practice*. Kluwer.

Awed, J., Elhajj, I.H., Chehab, A., & Kayssi, A. (2013). Perception-aware packet-loss resilient compression for networked haptic systems. *Computer Communications*, *36*(15–16), 1621–1628. https://doi.org/10.1016/j.comcom.2013.06.006

Bamford, A. (2006). *The wow factor: Global research compendium on the impact of arts in education*. Waxmann Verlag GmbH.

Boavida, F., Cerqueira, E., Mauthe, A., Curado, M., Lua, E.K., & Leszczuk, M. (2013). Special section on human-centric multimedia networking: Guest editorial. *Computer Communications*, *36*, 1606–1607.

Dreyfus, H.L. (2005). Overcoming the myth of the mental: How philosophers can profit from the phenomenology of everyday expertise. *Proceedings and Addresses of the American Philosophical Association*, *79*(2), 47–65.

Efland, A.D. (1990). *A history of art education: Intellectual and social currents of teaching the visual arts*. Teachers College Press.

Ehret, C., & Hollett, T. (2013). (Re)placing school: Middle school students' counter-mobilities while composing with iPods. *Journal of Adolescent & Adult Literacy*, *57*(2), 110–119.

Eisner, E.W. (2002). *The arts and the creation of mind*. Yale University Press.

Eisner, E.W. (2006). Does arts-based research have a future? *Studies in Art Education*, *48*(1), 9.

Høffding, S., & Snekkestad, T. (2021). Inner and outer ears: Enacting agential systems in music improvisation. In S. Ravn, S. Høffding, & J. McGuirk (Eds.), *The philosophy of improvisation: Interdisciplinary perspectives on theory and practice*. Routledge.

Kreimer, J. (2005). Adaptive detection of design flaws. *Electronic Notes in Theoretical Computer Science*, *141*(4), 117–136. https://doi.org/10.1016/j.entcs.2005.02.059

Langer, S. (1953). *Feeling and form: A theory of art*. Scribner.

Leander, K.M. (2015). *Essay 2: Educational design is out of time*. In G. Boldt, C. Lewis, & K.M. Leander. Moving, feeling, desiring, teaching. *Research in the Teaching of English*, *49*(4), 430–441.

McGuirk, J. (2021). Improvisation in the classroom: Towards an Aspectual Account of Improvisatory Practice. In S. Ravn & J. McGuirk (Eds.), *The philosophy of improvisation: Interdisciplinary perspectives on theory and practice.* Routledge.

Marner, A. (2013). Digital media embedded in Swedish art education – a case study. *Education Enquiry, 4*(2), 355–373. https://doi.org/10.3402/edui.v4i2.22078

Merleau-Ponty, M. (1962 [2012]). *Phenomenology of perception* (D. Landes, Trans.). Routledge.

Norman, D.A. (1988 [2013]). *The design of everyday things.* Basic Books.

Polanyi, M. (1969). *Knowing and being.* University of Chicago Press.

Saethre-McGuirk, E.M. (2021). An i for an eye: The collective shaping of experience in the age of machine-mediated art. In M. La Caze & T. Nannicelli (Eds.), *Truth in visual media: Aesthetics, ethics and politics.* Edinburgh University Press.

Shanahan, M. (2016). The frame problem. In E. N. Zalta (Ed.), *The Stanford encyclopedia of philosophy.* https://plato.stanford.edu/archives/spr2016/entries/frame-problem/

Zapata, A., Van Horn, S., Moss, D., & Fugit, M. (2019). Improvisational teaching as being with: Cultivating a relational presence toward justice-oriented literacies. *Journal of Adolescent & Adult Literacy, 63*(2), 179–187.

5 Pedagogical artistic research in the post-digital era

Art pedagogy research positions

Over the past quarter-century or so, art education has addressed the inclusion of new media and new technology into the fold, emphasising the use of new technology for art's, not technology's, purposes (cf. Burton, 2001; Choi & Piro, 2009; Delacruz, 2009; Freedman, 1997). Following from this, the question of how best to prepare preservice teachers for new, media-rich creative arts teaching situations has naturally been raised (cf. Roland, 2010), and consequently, critical discussions followed concerning why in-service art teachers refrained from including newer technologies in the art education classroom. It seems that the uneasy relationship between the digital and the physical or traditional in the creative arts has been linked to a number of practical challenges, such as time available and crowded curriculums, inadequate resources and training, professional and technical support, and practical access and restrictions (Bastos, 2010; Choi & Piro, 2009; Cuban, 2001; Delacruz, 2009; Gregory, 2009; Henning, 2000; Peppler, 2010; Wang, 2002; Wilks et al., 2012). Bearing in mind the national and political nature of education, others also identified countries' economic standing as indicative of how new media and technology, such as film, photography, media studies, and digital art and design, was embraced (Bamford, 2006).

Nonetheless, art education teachers, practitioner-researchers, and researchers of practice have long grappled with making and teaching in the digital era, fluctuating between understanding making from different positions and wavering between definitions of what the essential and non-essential differences in working in real and digital space are. These positions reflect different understandings of the relationship between the digital media-based and physical or materials-based art practice, and what that means for the pupil (and teacher). These positions simultaneously reflect the general development of education's relationship with personal computers from the late

DOI: 10.4324/9780429326264-5

1970s and early 1980s, when information and communication technology in earnest spread throughout education. This is seen, for example, in the initial interest in teaching children how to program, when 'thousands of schools taught millions of students how to write programs' (Resnick, 2012, p. 42).

Within education in art, the transition from late 1970s and early 1980s to the ever-greater inclusion of computers spurred different approaches to and levels of acceptance of digital space, even digital space in its very early forms. Not all were necessarily positive, and, indeed, as Anders Marner confirmed, 'digital media's entry into education can be conceived as filled with tension' (Marner, 2013, p. 356). The tension-filled relationship with new media and new technology wasn't necessarily only found in art education. Looking back on Seymour Papert's 1971 educational vision for what children could do with computers, Mitchel Resnick commented that although computers 'cost tens of thousands of dollars, if not more' in 1971 and were yet not commercially available, Papert foresaw that they would become available for everyone, including children, necessitating an intellectual foundation on which they could guide children in using these new tools (Resnick, 2012, p. 42). Alas, stuck on the difficulties of learning to programme and the instrumental techniques, as they were, schools eventually took computers into service for other aims than the designing, creating, and other powerful ideas that Papert had foreseen, making computers mere tools for delivering and accessing information and programming a 'narrow, technical activity, appropriate for only a small segment of the population' (Resnick, 2012, p. 42).

As a way to understand these early perspectives on a metalevel, we can group the different approaches together in three different and loosely defined approaches to digital space. These are derivative, delineated, and merged understandings of making in digital space, where working in the real and the digital are thought to negate, tangent, or complement each other, respectively. A greater understanding of these positions allows us to appreciate what challenges teachers and teaching communities saw themselves as meeting, in light of engaging their pupils in this way with these new technologies.

Practical challenges were only one reason that art educators were hesitant to see new technologies and to include them in their work with pupils. The use of digital technologies in visual art education in and of themselves was identified as problematic, with some citing materials and the ideology or framework of visual art as significant reasons (Choi & Piro, 2009; Hicks, 1993; Matthew et al., 2002; Phelps & Maddison, 2008). This position identified materiality as an undeniable and essential aspect of art and art education. As such, the digital was thought of as a derivative area of action; where digital making happens outside of and is different from working in the real, having mostly, if not only, essential differences from the ideology of creative arts education.

But, as Phelps and Maddison (2008) noted, creative arts teachers are as diverse in their relationship with new technology as teachers of other subjects are (Phelps & Maddison, 2008, p. 12). Therefore, it should also be noted that some teachers and researchers at the same time pointed to the possibilities that lay in the use of new technology, often emphasising the characteristics of visual communication and design and potential gains in light of artistic decision making, self expression, and creativity (Brown, 2002; Freedman, 1991; Hubbard & Greh, 1991; Long, 2001; Matthews, 1997; Stankiewicz, 2004; Wang, 2002; Wood, 2004). This position identified other essential aspects of the act of making things, in addition to or even in lieu of materiality. In accordance with this position, the digital was not a separate, derivative area of action; it was a delineated area of action where working in and with digital space and the real could coexist and positively contribute to individual and co-creative making. Some researchers even imagined the 'possibilities of calling attention to the potential of problem finding and problem solving for restructuring and enhancing transformations of creativity, technology, and pedagogy in art education' (Tillander, 2011, p. 46), through such an inclusive understanding of art and art education. As opposed to being a derivative area of action, it would seem that this position recognises making in digital space as delineated within artistic space. Though both essential and non-essential differences between digital and real space existed, essential similarities between the two were present and could be expanded on.

While research in art education often looked at how new technologies existed as separate from or were detrimental to the possibilities of art education within the traditional paradigm of art and art education, more recent research has looked at how the two fields of action are merged together in contemporary practice and education. This merged position has allowed an approach that accepts that the digital infiltrates culture, creativity, and society. Even art education in itself as an area of study could be thought to have been expanded by the ubiquitous nature of new technologies; with this, the traditional paradigm of art and art education can be opened up, no longer merely looking at what happens in formal education, but also looking at how non-formal and informal educational spheres also positively contribute to this merged area of action (cf. Black et al., 2015). Both a wider understanding of art education and formal education has made way for post-digital art education research and teaching. For example, Sakr (2017) studied early childhood education, creative arts, and digital technologies, citing how the pervasive nature of digital technologies was important to early childhood art, as through digital technologies children's art could be understood as 'an act of cultural production, through which [children] actively make themselves and the kinderculture that surrounds them' (Sakr, 2017, p. 181). Comparable findings were also brought forth by Sakr et al. (2018), where they emphasised the opportunities of expressive meaning making offered by the use of digital technologies. In this, we find a position which ultimately counteracts both the derivative and delineated approaches, and which rather makes room for a wide, merged approach holding that the digital further substantiates an existing art praxis and art education. In effect, asserting that there are no essential, only non-essential differences in working in digital and real space.

From the basis of this merged position, a more inclusive and flexible art education practice in the classroom can, if not must, evolve; one which is closer to the pupils' own concepts of reality (cf. Efland, 1990, p. 257), exemplified, for example, by Anders Marner's case study at one media-based school in Sweden:

> The pupils do not always choose to work either digitally or manually but like to combine the two methods. Combinations of digital and manual work are the most common working method. With regard to digital image creation, one girl thinks, "The teacher encourages it, but he does not say that we should do so". Another girl in the same groups adds, "No, it depends a lot on what you want to do".
>
> (Marner, 2013, p. 361)

The question is how to further foster this practice. There is clearly a need for in-service teacher training and education (Marner, 2013, p. 363) to better equip the teachers with the technical skills to be with the pupils in their making process, as has also been discussed here. What is more, concrete working methods in the classroom need not only support the improvisational microenvironment of the pupil, but they also need to be in harmony with the technical equipment available to the class, and that equipment must be suited for artmaking. Indeed, in Marner's case study, the interviewed teacher pointed to the fact that traditional computer rooms are not a 'natural' environment for artmaking (Marner, 2013, p. 359). Lastly, these concrete working methods demand sufficient time for this process to unfold. As any teacher would recognise, time is a valued commodity in the art classroom: both time for the pupils' processes and the time the teacher has with the individual pupils or groups of pupils.

Rethinking classroom practice in relation to making in digital space at the full expense of making with real tools and physical materials, though, would be a fool's errand. Not because of the importance of tradition and history or materials, but because the nature of the post-digital era demands that the pupils bring their experience of the world and making into that space.

Teaching making in digital space demands a holistic approach to learning in the creative arts. The implications of this in relation to early childhood education are profound, and that follows through in full but different ways throughout the pupils' formal educational settings, commencing at around 18 years of age. In this way, one can argue that art education can make possible new strides in more than the arts themselves, and not only make possible innovation by and through creatives. It comes as no surprise, then, that the discussion at hand intends to extend beyond the artist as maker, the pupil as maker, and the significance of digital space. It concerns a wide range of our actions in this new, expanded environment and isn't merely a creative arts education or art topic. It is one which concerns contemporary culture, knowledge, and innovation, and it is about essential discussions about being in the world.

This is so much the case that there are flipsides to this brief overview of perspectives on making things and teaching the creative arts in the post-digital era concerning human-computer interaction, digitalisation, and innovation. While our main argument at hand is an attempt at a critical, constructive understanding of making things in the interests of the creative arts and creative arts education, it is also relevant for a broad range of human-computer interaction studies and fields, from virtual reality developers to those developing digital surgeon's equipment and who are interested in the experience of the body and how it interacts through several layers of digital interfaces. The question remains, though, of how to further develop teaching the creative arts and education in art in the post-digital era in relation to research and pedagogical artistic research.

Professional identities and professional roles in the classroom

Continuing Papert's legacy, Resnick aimed at making programming more meaningful than before, finding the solutions to previously experienced shortcomings:

> We know that people learn best, and enjoy most, when they are working on personally meaningful projects. . . . We also . . . put a high priority on *personalization* – making it easy for people to personalize their . . . projects by importing photos and music clips, recording voices, and creating graphics.
>
> (Resnick, 2012, p. 43)

To achieve this, Resnick and his research group also created an online community, which they deemed as essential for the future success of their programming initiative, 'where people can support, collaborate, and critique one another and build on one another's work' (Resnick, 2012, p. 44). This is significant because, as Resnick pointed out, the online community constantly borrowed, adapted, and built on each other's work; so much so that more than a third of the work created there were remixes of other programming projects on the site (Resnick, 2012, p. 52).

It is not difficult to recognise parts of the arts classroom in these plans; that is, the emphasis on co-creation and reflection, recognising and reacting to aesthetic and non-aesthetic associations and references in making, and familiarity with different forms of digital space. Projects such as Resnick's reveal the transdisciplinary nature of the post-digital era, which, one would expect him to argue, closes the gaps between educational visions and coalface activity. And yet as we have seen in terms of the different meta-perspectives on including digital space and new media in the classroom, there are many practical reasons why this shift might not be as easily attained in all classrooms. A major issue that has yet to be discussed here, then, is how teaching practice in the classroom is closely tied to professional identity, outlooks on subject teaching and the role of the teacher, and, consequently, how professional development can find form in the greater landscape of the creative arts.

Note, though, that it would be wrong to speak of one community in this regard, in that teaching and planning take place within a conceptual, social, cultural, political, and historical framework, which is made more complex by the professional art education landscape of formal and non-formal art educators and the professional art sector. In addition, visual arts education draws on a number of fields and perspectives on art in general, such as, but not restricted to, visual culture, the history of art, emphasising skills in making processes, visual communication, multimodal teaching and learning, philosophy of art and art education, and art appreciation and museum education (Lindström, 2009, p. 17), in addition to overlapping areas made relevant by education through art. Many of these are their own subject fields, carrying with them, as it were, their own teaching traditions and approaches. The individual creative arts teacher's professional identity in the classroom will naturally reflect these different fields and perspectives in different ways, too.

Studying different professional identities inside the art education classroom, at the coalface, Anders Marner and Hans Örtegren (2013), looked into how the use of new technologies affected what teachers considered the core of creative arts education, which for the purpose of their article they dubbed 'the sacred'. Correspondingly, that which contradicted the sacred was dubbed 'the profane'. Although comprised of several individual communities on a greater scale, it would seem that smaller local and national communities share a common paradigm of what it entails to identify as a creative arts teacher, which develops and fully reveals itself in the class-room setting. In Marner and Örtegren's study, this common identity was mostly found to be strongly connected to the object and the physical making of that object:

> Art education is largely connected to the tools and materials used in the subject . . ... [They] are accompanied by a powerful tradition and history, linked to a traditional concept of art where the genius of the artist is in focus and to places where art is made and shown, for example studios, museums and galleries.
>
> (Marner & Örtegren, 2013, p. 674).

Dealing with the digital assumed a change which in and of itself was problematic, because it disturbed the individual's understanding of the sacred and the profane. Not because of their professional interest in tools and materials alone, but because of how tools and materials were intricately linked to both teaching and practice in the tradition and history that follow a professional visual arts educator identity. Therefore, it would seem that, while tradition and history are not necessarily brought to the fore in the classroom in the concrete lesson plans, they are there nonetheless, quite possibly as a common foundation that the diverse professional identities can converge at and approach the classroom from.

On the basis of their analysis, Marner and Örtegren then defined four different pedagogical approaches to the implementation of digital media into creative arts education in the classroom that reflected this sacred – profane paradigm: resistance, add-on, embeddedness, and digital media as dominant. These pedagogical approaches mirror the positions identified by the art researchers, apart from digital media as dominant. In this, they asked if digitalisation is or can be the future of creative arts education, or if it entails a change to the creative arts education paradigm on a metalevel which was simply too great a change (Marner & Örtegren, 2013, p. 671). Furthermore, Marner and Örtegren's work is interesting when looking at art education practice in the classroom and working in and with digital space in the post-digital era, because they not only confirm the underlying tension that existed between working with digital and physical materials, but also because they reveal how the different positions coexisted amongst art educators, inadvertently linking this to the professional field and its many arenas.

Undeniably, the same type of contradicting positions co-exist in the professional arts sector. While some fields firmly positioned within the wider category of art and design, such as architecture and industrial design, have long practiced in a digitalised creative field and participated in engaging in-depth thought about conception and perception in digital space (e.g. Marin et al., 2012), other professionals in those same fields nonetheless hold forth working in the real (e.g. Belardi, 2014). Specifically within contemporary visual art practice, though, one could argue that a merged approach to creative practice is well established in general (e.g. Kwastek, 2013) and within specific areas, too, such as with photographers and other artists, for example (e.g. Saethre-McGuirk, 2021; Saethre-McGuirk, 2022). Art practice researchers, such as Melissa Gronlund (2017), have taken on the status of art and art practice today through analyses of the internet, digital technologies, and art, and have studied how, particularly in contemporary art, artists have responded to central developments in new technology and to the internet as a mass cultural and socio-political medium. This link-up can be thought to extend from specific perspectives on ways of working, to the extent that some art practice as research has exclusively looked closer at the use and experience of sensory information in artistic, multimodal, and computer-based environments (e.g. Stenslie, 2010). Nonetheless, it would be misleading to state that this is so for the professional creative arts field as a whole. There is an overlapping, if not crisscrossing, presence of and relationship with the digital here, too. Art practice as research would seem to best address the current topic when the artist as researcher specifically studies art practice as a creative practice in the digital sphere, through the digital interface, as opposed to assuming that contemporary art has fully embraced digital space.

Following this, it is interesting to note that researchers in the arts have studied the digital and post-digital from several different approaches, such as from photography (Shapely, 2011) and portraiture (Altintzoglou, 2019), to film archives (Punt, 2005), sound (Pisano, 2015), and music (Cascone, 2000), and to narratives (Rasmussen, 2016) and the sacred (Hoff, 2017). Similarly, researchers have addressed major cross-disciplinary and interdisciplinary themes within these specific approaches (cf. La Caze & Nannicelli, 2021), thus deepening our understanding of digital space and the constitution of our actions there. Perhaps this is to be expected of creative arts's classroom practice in the post-digital era, then, where there is now room to critically address both digital space and analogue tools in the same breath, making more room for a more specific critical address of making in terms of teaching.

Research, teaching, and artistic practice

Understanding these different pedagogical approaches, research, and practices of implementing digital media into creative arts education is useful for conceptualising how digital space can be included in the visual art classroom. It also helps conceptualise the greater community the art teacher engages with. They also link up to the teacher's post-digital perspectives and competencies as part of the teacher's own practice-based research, too. And, while there are a multitude of ways the post-digital can show up in practice, it is useful to first exemplify what practice-based research can be, and secondly, to reflect in what that practice can make visible in relation to making in visual art. Magnus Wink, a university lecturer specialising in the creative arts school subject sloyd from Umeå University in Sweden, presented an artistic research project at a 2016 conference at the University of Turku, Finland, that can frame our further discussion about pedagogical artistic practice in the post-digital era.

In his presentation, Wink situated the session attendees in his university studio, where he had been working on different sloyd projects that included or touched upon digitalisation and new technologies. The main tool in his presentation was a MakeyMakey, a small, child and school friendly motherboard with alligator clips that you can link up to any object and, in effect, computerise the world. Seemingly intrigued by the possibilities of the MakeyMakey, Wink connected an alligator clip to his sloyd tools, one of which was an axe. Holding his alligator-clipped axe in one hand and attaching the other alligator-clip (somewhat painfully) to his other hand, Wink made his body an integral part of an axe-MakeyMakey loop. In addition, Wink set up a camera linked to the MakeyMakey through his computer, so that the camera formed its own loop together with the computer, taking input from the MakeyMakey and offering visual output to Wink through the computer screen. With the alligator-clipped axe in the one hand, and while supporting a fresh log of wood with the alligator-clipped hand, Wink went about splitting the log with the axe. Wink had programmed his computer to inform the camera to take a picture each time the axe head hit the wood, leading to picture after picture of wood shavings and chunks of log cracking and flying off the log that was carefully supported by his hand.

Wink explained his development process in detail, including his findings concerning the sharpness of the axe bit and the freshness of the wood; the axe bit had to be quite sharp, and the log had to be very fresh and contain lots of moisture for the circuit loop to work. But no matter how sharp the axe bit and how fresh the wood was, there was a constant lag between the instant the axe bit hit the wood and the picture was taken. What is more, to the conference audience's worry, there was seemingly always the chance of the axe bit missing the wood. Following that, Wink had to be careful not to hit the log too close to his hand, thus disrupting the loop. And losing a finger.

Through this project, Wink had incorporated his body as an action component in the loop, in effect making his whole body an integral part of the human-computer interaction project. The project had a clear digital component. Not the existence of the human-computer aspect in and of itself, but the fact that the output as photographic images came into being because of this loop.

As a sloyd practitioner, working with wood was an everyday interaction for Wink, and as with most everyday actions, Wink's actions for him were mundane, executed for the most part within the familiar loop perception, decision-making, and motor action (cf. Papetti, 2013). As tantalisingly unusual as the project seemed for art researchers because of its quirkiness, Wink's axe project was also interesting in how, in its simplicity, he skilfully tested the outer boundaries of the field of sloyd through digital tools. But most of all, it was interesting because it was explorative in relation to ways of making and seeing making happen. Wink fluctuated between directly engaging in splitting the wood and being able to watch himself split the wood on the computer screen, a few seconds after the act had taken place. In doing this, he moved the central locus of the act from his physical perception of using the axe and splitting the wood to the picture being taken (and shown), shifting the point of interest of the action and becoming his own audience, as it were. It's not the same as the free improvisation jazz musician being in the room with the audience and the music at the same time. Wink's project became a miniature mirroring event instead; that is, his own action directly followed by the presentation of the action which he could then see. Nearly, but not completely in real time, the action-presentation dialectic had the ability to become a type of self-other matching system, where the visual information presented to Wink (of himself as the other) could then inform his next action in a loop-like fashion, possibly changing the action of splitting the wood. Performing the act and then observing the act, Wink shared the making space and the emotional conditions connected to that act (cf. Foster, 2011) with both the conference presentation audience and himself. As such, with the possibility of watching himself perform, he could evaluate the predicted result and change his plan as it was unfolding. Not only was this part and parcel of an improvisational microenvironment in its own right; it was a practice-led research project in miniature, which could lead to new ideas about practice and have operational significance for himself and his students and their audience (Candy, 2006). His project was in effect an unpacking of everyday making action.

Importantly, Wink's project had exemplified how digital tools could be taken into service in art's exploring, experimenting, and testing boundaries, but more so, it was also an example of how new technology could be directly linked to flexible, creative thinkers (cf. Resnick, 2017, p. 3). As such, Wink had perhaps unintentionally illustrated what Papert's dream of expanding the conception of digital fluency to include designing and creating could be in practice (cf. Resnick, 2012, p. 46). However, Wink had not approached digital fluency and digital exploration from the perspective of digitalisation, computer science, or programming per se. Rather, Wink came at it from the perspective of the arts, finding resonance amongst this conference audience. Its quirkiness aside, Wink has exposed new layers of pedagogical artistic practice, using new technology and digital space to open doors to rooms of inquiry previously closed to us.

In retrospect, Wink's axe project did more than exemplify how digital space expands artistic space and, more importantly, pedagogical artistic space. It opened queries to how post-digital era pedagogical artistic competencies can develop and be better developed. The project left the conference room of art researchers with new ideas about how one could expand on this work as a starting point. Soon important epistemological questions arose: what kind of new knowledge had been generated or could be generated from projects such as these? And how could we link this up, so to speak, with creative arts teaching? Also, how does this research line up with research in the creative arts in pre-service teacher education?

In the group's discussions and answering of these questions after the session was over, it became clear that it was significant that Wink is a sloyd practitioner, overlapping the art and design divide through a seemingly shared procedural dimension that lends itself to formal inquiry in both fields (cf. Jones, 2006, p. 231). As such, Wink's project subsequently also exposed the substantial difference between the epistemological foundations of art and design. Whereas design and design research are 'associated with knowledge of and through use, and with the understanding of utilitarianism', art is more commonly 'associated with the exploration and understanding of the [human] consciousness' (Jones, 2006, p. 231) and closely related, deeply human areas of interest. Any understanding of what type of research projects could follow naturally reflected this difference as well. Understanding digital space as artistic space also reflected this difference. Looking more closely at digital space as artistic space for both art and design, we find that pedagogical artistic research is not merely interested in the creative arts product or in knowledge of and through use. Rather, like free improvisational jazz that has less of an interest in delivering a final product than in creating that product, pedagogical artistic research in art and design is interested in making processes, too. In contrast to the free improvisational jazz musician, pedagogical artistic research practice in visual art in particular is therefore interested in formal pedagogical situations in relation to children and young adults with the purpose of their exploring and understanding deeply human aspects of being.

Additional questions followed in the group, now tied to discussions concerning how pre-service teacher education could better equip their students to both conduct this type of pedagogical aesthetic research and utilise their and other researchers' findings in terms of pupil development, at the same time as accepting the differences of epistemological foundations in visual art and design. As traditional undergraduate and postgraduate courses have trained future university academic staff through research methods such as the traditional master's or PhD programme, it is clear that there is an expectation that those students will one day bring simplified forms of those research methods into their own classrooms (Jones, 2006, p. 231). In pre-service teacher education, however, there is an emphasis on pedagogy and children and youths, implying that the essential research and teaching that permeates those programmes is and must be pedagogical, and at that, pedagogical in terms of art. The underlying intention as such cannot be to prepare students to deliver a copy of the research perspective from pre-service teacher education in the classroom, but to prepare them for a teaching and research-active practice in the classroom, including unpacking shared procedural dimensions or with a focus on the epistemological foundations of art and design in its many forms (cf. Bamford, 2006). Pre-service teacher education in art is therefore not just concerned with practice related research. It must simultaneously be concerned with practice-led research, where the intention is to have operational significance, and practice-based research, where the creative artifact is itself the basis for the contribution of knowledge (Candy, 2006, p. 3).

This two-pronged concern informs the demands that exploration of digital space in a pedagogical setting place on the teacher. For the teacher to be able to be in digital space together with the pupil, to be able to recognise and to pursue emerging lines of flight towards the pupils' artmaking possibilities in digital space, implies both constructively including co-creative making processes and continuously developing professional knowledge. The art teacher's practice in the post-digital era is then that of a practice-based researcher. The teacher is active in the art processes, exploration, and research of the pupil, at the same time that they are concerned with their own practice-led research. Additionally, this complex research landscape is both site and temporally specific; it attends to the classroom, in real time, while teaching. As a pedagogical research situation, then, it is made all the more complex by the different layers of improvisatory action taking place at once in the act of teaching, through the teacher's and pupils' metaunderstanding of the act of making in digital space, and the practical making, within a pedagogical framework. As such, concrete demands are placed on teachers' pedagogical content knowledge, research competency, and art practice, enabling the pupils' constructive exploration of digital space, and enabling the pupils' navigation of digital space in terms of learning-in-time.

Looking now at Wink's axe project through the lens of arts-based educational research, where the aim is to address critical educational questions (e.g. Eisner, 2006), we can identify how the focus of the teacher's research interest both shifts over time through pre-service and in-service periods, and repositions itself according to the individual teacher's greater community of practice (cf. Eisner, 2002, p. 383). The problem with this, however, is twofold. Firstly, there has traditionally been a disconnect between the role of the teacher and the role of the artist. From an extreme point of view, while schools will often have teacher educated art teachers, some art staff in schools have been trained as and have professional careers as artists. In practice, higher education institutions can also employ professional artists as academic staff. This is not without its own kind of hardship linked to the dual professional identity of the artist and teacher: 'It seems the dual roles of artist and teacher have become increasingly difficult to combine in a world where both fields – art and education – are charged with expanding professional demands' (Jochum, 2015, p. 152). Teaching visual art in the post-digital era, though, clearly demands that these two roles become combined in the creative arts teacher. No longer merely a teacher teaching art or an artist teaching art, moving forward, the creative arts teacher must be at ease with both roles. Secondly, and more importantly, the arts-based educational research lens exposes the ingrained distinction between research-based and market-based artistic practice; thus putting into question how we judge the production of art objects and the objects themselves (Jones, 2006, pp. 228–229), as well as the professional skills of the artist. Negating an either-or perspective, though, one could argue that research-based artistic practice can in and of itself inform practice that is otherwise positioned towards the market, and as such, the art sector, as well as creative arts education.

To overcome these impediments to development in the field, research-based artistic practice with a palpable pedagogical anchoring must find its place in the greater landscape of art practice and research. Although there are several approaches and methodologies to art education research which could address these issues independently, one such approach is a/r/tography, defined as 'an inquiring process that lingers in the liminal spaces between a(*artist*) and r(*researcher*) and t(*teacher*)' (Springgay et al., 2005, p. 902). The multiple roles of the arts-based researcher are united in this approach, those being artist, researcher, and teacher; as such, the arts-based researcher is engaged in a methodology of embodiment, 'examining our personal, political and/or professional lives' (Gregory et al., 2021, p. 32). It has a particular reference to teacher education, drawing out the embedded ways of knowing in this overlapping and complex professional context (Pentassuglia, 2017, p. 2). From this viewpoint, one can explore 'phenomena through concepts rather than specific methods' and by looking closer at the 'process of constructing new knowledge, rather than following the specific criteria of an established research methodology' (Pourchier, 2010, p. 741). Furthermore, Stephanie Springgay et al. proposed a/r/tography as a means of research practice where one 'inquire[s] in the world through a process of art making and writing' (Springgay et al., 2005, p. 899). Through this, a/r/tography attempts to bring the boundaries between artmaking and research about art to an end (Springgay et al., 2005, p. 909).

Importantly, text and art do not in turn analyse one another through this research approach, but are constitutive; one voice, so to speak, 'in conversation *with*, *in*, and *through* art and text' (Springgay et al., 2005, p. 899). A/r/tography is a full and/and approach where text and art are explored as 'filled with potential in their juxtaposition', lending from Leander's comments in relation to improvisation as an analogy for understanding teaching (Leander, 2015, p. 437). In this, a/r/tography does not negate the text in its methodological approach to reach deeper understandings of phenomena through art. Indeed, Springgay et al. underline that both the image and the text 'need to be valued for the disciplinary and interdisciplinary traditions they represent' (Springgay et al., 2005, p. 903). Springgay et al. continue: 'It is a process of double imagining that includes the creation of art and words that are not separate or illustrative of each other but instead, are interconnected and woven through each other to create additional meanings' (Springgay et al., 2005, p. 899).

A/r/tographic work can be brought forth to identify possible emerging topics and perspectives in the art teacher's own practice-led research, which can also be understood in relation to the pupil and pupils and the co-creation that can happen in the classroom. Springgay et al. identify six 'renderings' that both inform and are informed by practice (Springgay et al., 2005), one of which, contiguity, is of special interest here. Contiguity places the a/r/tographer within the folds of their multiple identities, reminding us that this research is part of that

> . . . to live a contiguous life, a life that dialectically moves between connecting and not connecting the three roles. The dialectical in/between spaces amid these roles are dynamic living spaces of inquiry: Space touching at the edges, then shifting to be close, adjacent, but not touching – only to touch again.
>
> (Springgay et al., 2005, p. 901)

In this, contiguity as a rendering encourages citing and situating one's work within a larger conversation, a conversation which ultimately must include the pupil as well. This researcher engages in communities of practice, which in terms of pedagogical artistic research anchored in both pedagogy and the classroom includes the pupil, wherever the pupil or pupils may be in their work, in their double imaging; to better understand bodies of literature, visual landscapes, and being with in being in the world within and across multiple fields (cf. Pourchier, 2010, p. 741). However, it also acknowledges that a/r/tography is a living inquiry, that is, rendering a being in the world 'through constant reflection, contemplation, and theorizing that is explored through art, research, and teaching' (Pourchier, 2010, p. 741). Following this, the remaining four renderings (metaphor/metonymy, openings, excess, and reverberations) address how we make sense of the world through metaphors and metonyms, how one can stimulate dialogue through research, how provocation can lead to transformation, and how that research can turn around and stimulate new understandings of the phenomenon being studied (Springgay et al., 2005; Irwin & Springgay, 2008).

While the role of art in life remains fundamental to us as humans in the post-digital era, we can experience making in digital space as different to making in the real, even though there are no essential differences to the art process itself. It becomes the role of the teacher to guide the pupil into those spaces of making art. Furthermore, making in digital space and being attentive to the possibilities for artistic research in that space makes insight into aspects of making possible, which are otherwise not available to us. This can help us understand how pupils, with guidance from teachers and others, can go past the first strata of technical abilities and reach deeper into the perceptual techniques made available to them in digital space as artistic space, and overcome the non-essential yet important differences that do exist between unambiguous and ambiguous ecologies of making.

Bibliography

Altintzoglou, E. (2019). Digital realities and virtual ideals: Portraiture, idealism and the clash of subjectivities in the post-digital era. *Photography and Culture, 12*(1), 69–79. https://doi.org/10.1080/17514517.2019.1565290

Bamford, A. (2006). *The wow factor: Global research compendium on the impact of arts in education.* Waxmann Verlag GmbH.

Bastos, F. (2010). New media art education. *Art Education, 63*(1), 4–5.

Belardi, P. (2014). *What architects still draw* (Z. Nowak, Trans.). MIT Press.

Black, J., Castro, J.C., & Lin, C.C. (2015). *Youth practices in digital arts and new media: Learning in formal and informal settings.* Palgrave Macmillan.

Brown, I. (2002). New radicalism for art education: Embracing change. *Australian Art Education, 25*(1), 62–64.

Burton, D. (2001). How do we teach? Results of a national survey of instruction in art education. *Studies in Art-Education, 42*(2), 131–145.

Candy, L. (2006). *Practice based research: A guide; creativity & cognition studios.* University of Technology Sydney, CCS.

Cascone, K. (2000). The aesthetics of failure: "Post digital" tendencies in contemporary computer music. *Computer Music Journal, 24*(4), 12–18.

Choi, H., & Piro, J.M. (2009). Expanding arts education in a digital age. *Arts Education Policy Review, 110*(3), 27–34. https://doi.org/10.3200/AEPR.110.3.27-34

Cuban, L. (2001). *Oversold & underused: Computers in the classroom*. Harvard University Press.

Delacruz, E.M. (2009). Art education aims in the age of new media: Moving toward global civil society. *Art Education, 62*(5), 13–18. https://doi.org/10.1080/00043125.2009.11519032

Efland, A.D. (1990). *A history of art education: Intellectual and social currents of teaching the visual arts*. Teachers College Press.

Eisner, E. (2002). *The arts and the creation of mind*. Yale University Press.

Eisner, E. (2006). Does arts-based research have a future? Inaugural lecture for the first European conference on arts-based research, Belfast, Northern Ireland, June 2005. *Studies in Art Education: A Journal of Issues and Research, 48*(1), 9–18.

Foster, S.L. (2011). *Choreographing empathy*. Routledge.

Freedman, K. (1991). Possibilities of interactive computer graphics for art instruction: A summary of research. *Art Education, 44*(3), 41–47.

Freedman, K. (1997). Visual art/virtual art: Teaching technology for meaning. *Art Education, 50*(4), 6–12.

Gregory, D. (2009). Boxes with fire: Wisely integrating learning technologies into the classroom. *Art Education, 63*(3), 47–54.

Gregory, D., Fisher, J., & Leavitt, H. (2021). The impact of continual reflection students as partners: Becoming a/r/tographers. *The Journal of Scholarship of Teaching and Learning, 21*(1).

Henning, G. (2000). Introducing digital technologies into the year 9/10 visual arts program: Cooperative learning in action. *Australian Art Education, 23*(2), 37–41.

Hicks, J. (1993). Technology and aesthetic education: A critical synthesis. *Art Education, 46*(6), 42–47.

Hoff, J. (2017). The eclipse of sacramental realism in the age of reform: Rethinking Luther's Gutenberg galaxy in a post-digital age. *New Blackfriars, 99*(1080), 248–270. https://doi.org/10.1111/nbfr.12343

Hubbard, G., & Greh, D. (1991). Integrating computing into art education: A progress report. *Art Education, 44*(3), 18–24.

Irwin, R.L., & Springgay, S. (2008). A/r/tography as practice-based research. In S. Springgay, R. Irwin, C. Leggo, & P. Gouzouasis (Eds.), *Being with a/r/tography* (pp. xix–xxxiii). Sense.

Jochum, R. (2015). The changing education of the artist. In R. Mateus-Berr & M. Götsch (Eds.), *Perspectives on art education: Conversations across cultures*. De Gruyter.

Jones, T.E. (2006). The studio-art doctorate in America. *Art Journal, 65*(2), 124–127. https://doi.org/10.1080/00043249.2006.10791208

Kwastek, K. (2013). *Aesthetics of interaction in digital art*. MIT Press.

La Caze, M. & Nannicelli, T. (2021). *Truth in visual media: Aesthetics, ethics, and politics*. Edinburgh University Press.

Leander, K.M. (2015). Essay 2: Educational design is out of time. In G. Boldt, C. Lewis, & K.M. Leander. Moving, feeling, desiring, teaching. *Research in the Teaching of English, 49*(4), 430–441.

Lindström, L. (2009). Issues in visual arts education: A conceptual framework. In L. Lindström (Ed.), *Nordic visual arts education in transition: A research review* (pp. 13–35). Swedish Research Council.

Long, S. (2001). Multimedia in the art curriculum: Crossing boundaries. *Journal of Art and Design Education, 20*(3), 255–263.

Marin, P., Liveneau, P., & Blanchi, Y. (2012, January 15–17). *Digital materiality: Conception, fabrication, perception* [conference paper], Scaleless Seamless, Performing a Less Fragmented Architecture and Education.

Marner, A. (2013). Digital media embedded in Swedish art education – a case study. *Education Enquiry, 4*(2), 355–373. https://doi.org/10.3402/edui.v4i2.22078

Marner, A., & Örtegren, H. (2013). Four approaches to implementing digital media in art education. *Education Inquiry, 4*(4), 671–688. https://doi.org/10.3402/edui.v4i4.23217

Matthew, K., Callaway, R., Letendre, C., Kimbell-Lopez, K., & Stephens, E. (2002). Adoption of information communication technology by teacher educators: One-on-one coaching. *Journal of Information Technology for Teacher Education, 11*(1), 45–61.

Matthews, J. (1997). *Computers and art education.* The National Art Education Association.

Papetti, S. (2013, April 18–21). *Design and perceptual investigations of audio-tactile interactions* [conference paper], International Conference on Acoustics – AIA-DAGA.

Pentassuglia, M. (2017). 'The Art(ist) is present': Arts-based research perspective in educational research. *Cogent education, 4*(1).

Peppler, K. (2010). Media arts: Arts education for a digital age. *Teachers College Record, 112*(8), 2118–2153.

Phelps, R., & Maddison, C. (2008). ICT in the secondary visual arts classroom: A study of teachers' values, attitudes and beliefs. *Australasian Journal of Educational Technology, 24*(1), 1–14.

Pisano, L. (2015). The third soundscape: How a sonic exploration of abandoned spaces can lead to the discovery of unforeseen places and the geographies of a territory in the post-digital era. *Third Text, 29*(1–2), 75–87. https://doi.org/10.108 0/09528822.2015.1049888

Pourchier, N. (2010). Art as inquiry: A book review of being with a/r/tography. *Qualitative Report, 15*(3), 740–745. https://doi.org/10.46743/2160-3715/2010.1175

Punt, M. (2005). What the film archive can tell us about technology in the post-digital era. *Design Issues, 21*(2), 48–62.

Rasmussen, E.D. (2016). Narrative and affect in William Gillespie's keyhole factory and morpheus_ biblionaut, or, post-digital fiction for the programming era. *ComputerText, 2*(2), 140–171.

Resnick, M. (2012). Reviving Papert's dream. *Educational Technology, 52*(4), 42–46.

Resnick, M. (2017). *Lifelong kindergarten: Cultivating creativity through projects, passion, peers, and play.* MIT Press.

Roland, C. (2010). Preparing art teachers to teach in a new digital landscape. *Art Education, 63*(1), 17–24. https://doi.org/10.1080/00043125.2010.11519049

Sakr, M. (2017). *Digital technologies in early childhood art: Enabling playful experiences*. Bloomsbury Academic.

Sakr, M., Connelly, V., & Wild, M. (2018). Imitative or iconoclastic? How young children use ready-made images in digital arts. *International Journal of Art & Design Education, 37*(1), 41–52.

Saethre-McGuirk, E. (2021). An i for an eye: The collective shaping of experience in the age of machine mediated art. In M. La Caze & T. Nannicelli (Eds.), *Truth in visual media: Aesthetics, ethics, and politics* (pp. 58–76). Edinburgh University Press.

Saethre-McGuirk, E. (2022). Hvem tegner? In A.C. Hedberg & R. Lundgreen (Eds.), *Digital og analog tegning i museet* (pp. 11–31). Museumsforlaget.

Shapely, G. (2011). After the artifact: Post-digital photography in our post-media era. *Journal of Visual Art Practice, 10*(1), 5–20.

Springgay, S., Irwin, R.L., & Kind, S.W. (2005). A/r/tography as living inquiry through art and text. *Qualitative Inquiry, 11*(6), 897–912. https://doi.org/10.1177/1077800405280696

Stankiewicz, M. (2004). Notions of technology and visual literacy. *Studies in Art Education, 46*(1), 88–92.

Stenslie, S. (2010). *Virtual touch: A study of the use and experience of touch in artistic, multimodal and computer-based environments* [PhD thesis, The Oslo School of Architecture and Design].

Tillander, M. (2011). Creativity, technology, art, and pedagogical practices. *Art Education, 64*(1), 40–46. https://doi.org/10.1080/00043125.2011.11519110

Wang, L. (2002). How teachers use computers in instructional practice: Four examples in American schools. *Journal of Art and Design Education, 21*(2), 154–163.

Wilks, J., Cutcher, A., & Wilks, S. (2012). Digital technology in the visual arts classroom: An [un]easy partnership. *Studies in Art Education, 54*(1), 54–65. https://doi.org/10.1080/00393541.2012.11518879

Wood, J. (2004). Open minds and a sense of adventure: How teachers of art & design approach technology. *The International Journal of Art & Design Education, 23*(2), 179–191.

6 Conclusion

Challenges and possibilities

The aim of this book has been to gain a better understanding of making things and teaching the creative arts in the post-digital era. My emphasis has undeniably been on visual art, inviting future in-depth study in the other creative arts, which may indeed result in fruitful comparisons for deeper insight into the creative arts as a whole, as well as for related cross-disciplinary fields in our post-digital era. I have attempted to draw a line from understanding the role and purpose of art, not only from making and art processes in general to teaching, but to meta-level reflections on arts-based pedagogical research as well. As such, I have had two main objectives. The first has been to critically address what happens during processes of conceptualising, constructing, and giving form to objects in the real and through a digital interface, and, through that, gaining a greater understanding of the teaching related implications of these processes as they take shape in the post-digital era. The second has been to delineate a more productive understanding of the process of making things through a digital interface, accepting that those processes are not merely one-way (human-to-computer), but have a retroactive effect on the person who is making the object (computer-to-human), as well as on the act of making in an art process itself.

I took as my starting point a personal account of the aesthetic practice of making and the role of materiality. It was first through in-depth phenomenological reflection on the act of drawing that I began to study these issues in earnest. Through my practical exploratory work, I found there to be differences between making in digital two-dimensional and three-dimensional space and making in the real that hadn't been discussed in full from both a creative arts perspective and, following that, from a teaching perspective. The differences themselves are non-essential in terms of making in post-digital artistic space, even though they come across as important in the act of making. They do so because I am dependant on my physical experiences

DOI: 10.4324/9780429326264-6

of materials to also learn about my body when making and my being in the world through my senses. Upon realising that these differences have an impact on how I teach art and teach future teachers of art, I found there was a need to further unpack what it means to make and teach art in the post-digital era.

In this, I simultaneously recognise the enormous potential that lays in better understanding these processes of making and teaching. This potential is not first and foremost an economic one, in light of national and inter-national digitalisation and innovation strategies, although it is clearly that as well. This potential is primarily understood as the benefits it offers the pupil. Making art is a fundamental human practice and the role of art in life comes into play in helping us make sense of the world and at the same time enabling us to reconceptualise ourselves in the world - also a world where digital space figures. Ideas come from art. Understanding comes from art. And subsequently, innovation and change come from art.

In that teaching is planned and takes place within a conceptual, social, cultural, political, and historical framework, the underlying understanding of this role is determinative for how making in digital space and teaching the creative arts in the post-digital era will find its form at the coalface. For this reason, it is in the interest of national and international policymakers to carefully consider the nuances of the different roles they want the creative arts to have, as they will affect the outcome. The motivation for new outcomes should not be confused with the route to get there. An aim of better positioning education to foster children, youths, and young adults to take risks and try new things, define new problems, create new directions, and come up with innovative ideas – in short, to develop their own ideas, goals, and strategies (cf. Resnick, 2017, p. 3) – in terms of digitalisation and inno-vation through new technologies and media, isn't necessarily best achieved by simply giving them more digital tools. Such a pedagogical approach is reminiscent of getting out of the child's way by providing pupils with equipment and exploratory opportunities, and assuming that their innova-tive capacities will be released and substantial education will be the result (cf. Eisner, 2002, p. 233). Elliot Eisner called this 'a kind of pedagogy by neglect' (Eisner, 2002, p. 233), criticising a widespread tendency in relation to education in art. Indeed, it would seem the same can often be said in rela-tion to digitalisation and innovation strategies.

At the same time, this is not to say that technology in schools, if properly designed, supported, and used in an educational framework, is a task almost certain to fail, because it is not. Neither is it wasteful to teach through the creative arts and visual art to achieve educational goals relating to digi-talisation and technology strategies, both in the arts classroom and in other subjects. It is important to be cognisant of significant findings that show that education through art, which uses creative and artistic pedagogies in the classroom to teach all curricula, may indeed enhance overall academic attainment, reduce school disaffection, and promote positive cognitive transfer (Bamford, 2006, p. 12), including learning in line with digitalisation and technology strategies. However, it should be noted that was found to only be beneficial where there were provisions of quality education through arts programmes; poor-quality programmes were found to actively inhibit those benefits (Bamford, 2006, p. 12). Furthermore, there are indications that there is a robust link between arts-rich general educational programming and the widespread and creative use of information and communication technologies (Bamford, 2006, p. 138).

This is to say, then, that for national and international digitalisation and innovation policy to succeed at the coalface, we need both education through the arts and education in the arts. That is, creative arts education must also unfold on its own terms, and not only be in service of other purposes. This education in the arts with a focus on making in both the real and in digital space looks past binary divisions and dichotomies of the real versus the digital; it sees making art and articulation of import as one activity and is at the same time aware of the experienced differences between those spaces where making happens, and the pedagogical implications that follow. It invites a technological use-non-use, in an and/and setting. It is interesting to look at the language we use about making in this regard. Where we once, for example, just spoke of photography in relation to taking a picture because that is what it was, we would eventually take to saying digital photography, and in recent years artists working with photography as a medium now specify analogue photography as their medium, in that digital photography has become the norm from which they want to differentiate themselves. While there is certainly a significant difference between digital and analogue photography, it is first when we use both terms on equal terms – or, consequently, just photography – that we can sense that we have finally moved on from the digital era's reactionary stance against the universal machine.

It might seem contradictory, then, that I insist on defining digital space, and not just present it as artistic space. The reason for my approach is that digital space must be understood on its own grounds, precisely as digital photography offers something that analogue photography cannot. To ignore those important but non-essential differences would similarly be a pedagogy by neglect. Understanding those grounds in full and in their own right is necessary, in respect of the tools, materials, and space as they show up to me in the act of making, to pupils as they learn to navigate that space, and to teachers as they navigate that space with their pupils. It is also necessary to understand those grounds in full for teaching future teachers; that is, in pre-service teacher education, as well as for teaching those in early child-hood education programmes and in art programmes planning to take on teaching roles in non-formal education. Lastly, it is necessary for position-ing in-service teachers to be able to develop their own research-based per-spectives on teaching in this space, being with pupils as artists, researchers, and teachers, through in-service teacher education programming.

Those grounds reveal an artistic space that demands a pedagogy of co-creation, constructive exploration, and participation in the pupil's improvi-satory microenvironment. It also demands a developed aesthetic awareness of the world. Its rewards fold back into making in the real, enabling pupils to think new thoughts and think sideways about old problems. In this sense, education in art - that is, in the creative arts in the post-digital era - is not just the missing piece, as it were, for digitalisation and innovation programmes to fully succeed; it is the fundament which makes that success possible. And yet, the raison d'être of creative arts education is not to simply be that foun-dation. It is the seed from which a plant with many different fruits grows, not just the cherries that have been picked from it.

The significance of this has been under communicated to or can easily be misunderstood by those who have no concern of digitalisation and innova-tion programmes and policy, and perhaps only want to promote education in art for the sake of education in art. Their priorities are right, because an instrumentalisation of the creative arts for external purposes would under-mine this foundation. At the same time, the possibilities that follow work-ing in digital space in an art educational context should not be reduced or put aside for developing office-based skills, nor should they be neglected in terms of necessary software access or advice in light of the role of new technology in art education. The professional attitude towards working in this space and what it entails needs to be situated amongst the teachers in the classroom, but also, importantly, in the school as a whole, including its leadership levels, and in the administrative levels above that.

As we situate ourselves in the post-digital era, digital space will become an even more fruitful arena to engage in making, understanding, and inter-acting. Space augmented digitally to different degrees especially will become a fertile space for a vast range of industry, as well as society as a whole, placing an even greater emphasis on creative arts education and its ability to cultivate being in this space, making in this space, and thinking in this space as a baseline competency. Therefore, while contemporary policy intended to unite creatives and technology is a good first step, it does not go far enough in the greater scale of things in lifting the bar wholesale in sup-porting transdisciplinary arenas and efforts.

For this shift to fully take form in and through creative arts education, we depend on two main features unfolding. Firstly, we need to ensure room for the detailed study of practical, professional knowledge in a research framework. This entails not only accepting that humanities research is full advanced research that is at once both fundamental to our understanding of that practical, professional knowledge, as well as to our being in the world and changing the world through innovation. It also entails accepting that that arts-based research can offer necessary insight into complex relational, improvisatory actions and understandings, which can further clarify that which the humanities has otherwise uncovered. It follows that the humanities and arts cannot just find space in our educational programmes in schools and universities, as well as in our pre-service teacher education programmes; they need to be actively supported, promoted, and funded on an institutional and national level.

Secondly, this places a significant responsibility on the shoulders of the teacher, especially the art teacher. There are significant implications that follow this in terms of the teacher's pedagogical content knowledge in art, drawing on the intricate self-knowledge of the teacher, accepting all of the roles of the teacher at once: the artist, the researcher, the teacher. In this, I suggest an a/r/tography methodology as one of many arts-based educational research means to fully unpack making in digital space in the post-digital era within educational research. From my perspective of author and maker, this written work also has corresponding practical bodies of work, with a research-based artistic practice with it at its core. Having used these bodies of work to start a discussion about how and why we make things, leading to an understanding of what the essential qualities of art are, we could then move our attention to materials before addressing digital space. To develop this work even further, though, we need more insight from the practical field. Central to our understanding of this space, how the pupils negotiate this space as an improvisatory microenvironment, and how teachers address that negotiation, is the understanding that teachers must be active researchers in their field, securing their own meta-reflection about making and teaching in that space, as well as participating in a community of artists, researchers, and teachers and in the school as a community of learning.

In such a light and in the greater context of making things, digital space and human-computer interaction is one of many ways of making, but meeting that space on its own terms is simultaneously a chance to reboot how we conceptualise the creative arts in their own right and their place in schools and education. Understanding the unique phenomenology of aesthetic practice within the post-digital era makes change on a greater scale not only possible but also, I argue, likely to succeed. What is more, understanding aesthetic practice in digital space for pedagogical purposes in the post-digital era underlines the aesthetic, communicative, and co-creative core of the creative arts. Making room for distinct but still fundamentally human ways of thinking, positioning, and repositioning ourselves in the world, and for the pupils' developing ways of thinking of themselves in this world.

Our post-digital era is panoptic and understanding digital space as part of an artistic space in this way, with its all-encompassing nature, offers valuable insight and advances for the digital transformation of society, the innovative reuse of existing technologies, and the rewarding link between creatives and others. In this sense, the post-digital era is one where the field has become intradisciplinary, making teaching the creative arts in the post-digital era arguably increasingly important.

Bibliography

Bamford, A. (2006). *The wow factor: Global research compendium on the impact of arts in education*. Waxmann Verlag GmbH.

Eisner, E.W. (2002). *The arts and the creation of mind*. Yale University Press.

Resnick, M. (2017). *Lifelong kindergarten: Cultivating creativity through projects, passion, peers, and play*. MIT Press.

Index

.

Milton Keynes UK
Ingram Content Group UK Ltd.
UKHW022040190124
436364UK00007B/99